This book attempts to uncover the basic form and structure of the Babylonian Talmud, a centrally important text in Jewish studies. The novel contribution made by Dr Jacobs to the study of the Talmud consists in his concentration on the literary principles employed in its composition, and he here presents a clear survey indicating the manner in which earlier material was reworked in order to make each component, or *sugya*, into a carefully structured and self-consistent unit. Comparatively little work has been done hitherto on why the Babylonian Talmud has been shaped and structured in the way it has. By examining a number of Talmudic passages, and subjecting them to close analysis, this book arrives at important conclusions, and shows, for example, that the Talmud is an academic, rather than a practical work; that it is largely pseudepigraphic; and that it is the result of a sustained literary activity.

Structure and form in the
Babylonian Talmud

Structure and form in the Babylonian Talmud

LOUIS JACOBS

Visiting Professor in Jewish Thought,
Department of Religious Studies,
Lancaster University

CAMBRIDGE UNIVERSITY PRESS

Cambridge

New York   Port Chester   Melbourne   Sydney

Published by the Press Syndicate of the University of Cambridge
The Pitt Building, Trumpington Street, Cambridge CB2 1RP
40 West 20th Street, New York, NY 10011-4211, USA
10 Stamford Road, Oakleigh, Melbourne 3166, Australia

First published 1991

Printed in Great Britain at the University Press, Cambridge

British Library cataloguing in publication data
Jacobs, Louis
Structure and form in the Babylonian Talmud.
1. Judaism. Talmud — Critical studies
I. Title
296. 12506

Library of Congress cataloguing in publication data
Jacobs, Louis
Structure and form in the Babylonian Talmud/Louis Jacobs.
p.   cm.
Includes bibliographical references.
ISBN 0 521 40345 6 (hardcover)
1. Talmud — Criticism. Redaction. I. Title.
BM503.6.J28 1991
296. 1'206 — dc20 90–2669   CIP

ISBN 0 521 40345 6 hardback

For
Jack, Alex, Marga, Hadiyah, Peter and Anita,
close relatives and even closer friends

Contents

Preface

This book is an attempt to uncover the basic form and structure of the Babylonian Talmud. While a number of modern scholars have called attention to the fairly obvious fact that its final editors have used earlier material for their construction, little note has been taken of the way in which this material has been reworked so as to make each *sugya* a carefully structured unit, much as, say, Shakespeare's plays have converted the chronicles he used into a totally different and far more dramatic literary form.

Chapters 1 and 2 discuss the general nature of the Babylonian Talmud, pointing to the pseudepigraphic and purely academic form of a good deal of the material. Chapter 3, on Rabbinic views regarding the order and authorship of the Biblical books, has its place here both because of the light it sheds on the structure of a *sugya* and because it provides some indication of how the Rabbis thought literary units were compiled in ancient times. Chapters 4 through to 8 attempt an analysis of particular *sugyot* on the lines I have tried in my books, *Studies in Talmudic Logic and Methodology* (London, 1961) and *The Talmudic Argument* (Cambridge, 1984). Chapters 9 and 10 compare the treatment of particular narratives in the Babylonian and Jerusalem Talmuds, from which the tendency of the Babylonian Talmud to shape its material in a more dramatic form than the Jerusalem Talmud becomes clear. A cogent illustration of editorial method is provided in the stories about R. Banaah treated in chapter 11. Chapter 12 examines a literary device used by the editors of the Babylonian Talmud in presenting the material so that each item appears at just the right moment.

None of these studies has appeared elsewhere except for chapter 1, an earlier version of which appeared in the *Journal of Jewish Studies* (Spring, 1977), pp. 46–59, for which I thank the editor.

Abbreviations

ARN	*Avot de-Rabbi Natan*
'Arukh	Talmudic dictionary by Nathan of Rome (1035–*c.* 1110)
b.	*ben,* 'son of'
Baḥ	*Bayit Ḥadash* by Joel Sirkes (1561–1640)
BT	Babylonian Talmud
CE	Common Era
DS	*Dikdukey Soferim* by R. Rabbinovicz
EJ	*Encyclopaedia Judaica*
ET	*Entziklopedia Talmudit*
Gilyon ha-Shas	Notes of R. Akiba Eger (1761–1837)
ha-Gra	Notes of Elijah Gaon of Vilna (1720–97)
HUCA	*Hebrew Union College Annual*
JE	*Jewish Encyclopaedia*
JT	*Jerusalem Talmud*
JJS	*Journal of Jewish Studies*
Maharsha	Novellae of R. Samuel Edels (1555–1631)
Meiri	Commentary of R. Menahem Meiri of Perpignan (1249–1316)
R.	Rabbi
Raabad	R. Abraham Ibn David of Posquirés (d. 1198)
Ran	R. Nissim Gerondi (*c.* 1235–*c.* 1375)
Rashba	R. Solomon Ibn Adret (d. *c.* 1310)
Rashbam	R. Samuel b. Meir (d. *c.* 1174)
Rashi	R. Solomon Yitzhaki (1040–1105)
Reshash	R. Samuel Strashun (1794–1872)
Rif	Code of R. Yitzhak Alfasi (1013–1103)
Ritba	R. Yom Tov Ishbili (d. 1330)
Soncino	English translation of the Babylonian Talmud, Soncino Press

The Babylonian Talmud: an introductory note

Although this book is a technical study of a complex literary work, it is hoped that it will be of interest to non-specialists in the field as well as to Talmudic scholars. This note provides a brief sketch of the background and the technical terms used for the benefit of readers who come to the subject without any prior knowledge.

In the scheme developed in Rabbinic Judaism, the doctrine of the Oral Torah (*Torah she-be-'al peh*) looms very large. According to this doctrine, Moses received at Sinai a detailed elaboration of the laws and doctrines contained in the Pentateuch, the Written Torah (*Torah she-bikhetav*). The Oral Torah embraces, too, the later teachings of the Sages and teachers of Israel as a continuing process. Especially during the first two centuries of the present era, the teachings of the Oral Torah were discussed and debated (an essential feature in the whole process at this period is argument on the correctness or incorrectness of this or that opinion) by the Tannaim (sing. Tanna, from the Aramaic root *teni*, 'to teach'), although this name was only given to them later. In their own day the Tannaim were usually referred to as the Sages (*hakhamim*). Among the more important of the Tannaim were: the rival Houses of Hillel and Shammai; Rabban Johanan ben Zakkai; Rabbi Eliezer; Rabbi Joshua; Rabbi Akiba and his disciples, Rabbi Meir, Rabbi Judah, Rabbi Simeon; and, another Judah, Rabbi Judah the Prince. As his title Prince (*Nasi*) implies, this Rabbi Judah was the political as well as spiritual leader of his people with a degree of autonomy granted to him by the Roman government. Possessing the requisite authority, Rabbi Judah the Prince was able to collect the teachings and debates of the Tannaim to form a digest of the Oral Torah. This work is known as the Mishnah (from the root *shanah*, 'to teach') and was compiled by Rabbi Judah the Prince at the end of the second, beginning of the third century CE. The Mishnah was composed in Hebrew, the scholarly language of the period, and is divided into the six Orders:

1

1 *Zera'im*, 'Seeds' (agricultural laws)
2 *Mo'ed*, 'Appointed Time' (Sabbath and Festival laws)
3 *Nashim*, 'Women' (laws of marriage and divorce)
4 *Nezikin*, 'Damages' (torts, buying and selling, jurisprudence in general)
5 *Kodashim*, 'Sanctities' (laws of the sacrificial system in the Temple)
6 *Tohorot*, 'Purities' (the laws of ritual contamination and the means of purification)

The Orders of the Mishnah are divided into tractates (*masekhtot*) and these subdivided into chapters. Each chapter (*perek*) is made up of smaller units, *mishnayot* (plural of *mishnah*). Thus the term *mishnah* is used of the work as a whole and of its smallest unit; each of these being a 'teaching', and the work as a whole the teaching of Rabbi Judah the Prince.

The Hebrew of the Mishnah is consequently known as Mishnaic Hebrew. A good deal of the material (the last two Orders, for example) was of no practical significance for Jewish religious life since it deals with conditions in Temple times. Rabbi Judah the Prince compiled the Mishnah around the year 220 CE and the Temple was destroyed in the year 70 CE. Evidently, the aim of Rabbi Judah the Prince and his associates was to provide a complete digest of the whole of the Oral Torah irrespective of its practical relevance. To study the Torah was a supreme religious aim in itself quite apart from its practical consequences.

The Mishnah is not the only source of Tannaitic teachings. There are, in addition, the Tosefta, 'Supplement' to the Mishnah; the Mekhilta, 'Measure', on the Biblical book of Exodus, the Sifra, 'the Book', on Leviticus, also called *Torat Kohanim*, 'The Law of the Priests', and Sifré, 'the Books', on Numbers and Deuteronomy. These last three are known as the Halakhic Midrashim or the Tannaitic Midrashim. Other Tannaitic teachings are found in sources quoted in the Talmud known as *baraitot* (sing. *baraita*; the word means 'outside', i.e. teachings not included in the Mishnah).

Once the Mishnah had won acceptance as a canonical text, the teachers in both Palestine and Babylon devoted most of their efforts to its elucidation; hence the name by which these teachers came to be known — Amoraim, 'Expounders' of the Tannaitic teachings. The scholarly activity the Amoraim engaged in was largely in Aramaic, though, naturally, many of the legal maxims and quotes from earlier sources were in Hebrew. The Palestinian Amoraim used the western Aramaic dialect, the Babylonians the eastern dialect.

An introductory note

Around the year 400 CE, the teachings, debates and discussions that took place among the Palestinian Amoraim were drawn on to form the Palestinian Talmud, also known as the *Yerushalmi* ('of Jerusalem'), although no Jews actually lived in Jerusalem in this period. There has been much discussion on the question of who the editors of the *Yerushalmi* were. There is evidence, stylistic and historical, that some sections of the *Yerushalmi* were edited earlier, and in a different centre, than others. The style of the *Yerushalmi* is, in any event, terse and, it might be said, 'choppy', so that some scholars have suggested that the work never received any final redaction and is incomplete.

A similar process of redaction took place in Babylon around the year 500 CE (the date is very approximate) to form the Babylonian Talmud, the *Bavli*. The style of the *Bavli* is much more elaborate than that of the *Yerushalmi* and, apart from a few tractates, is uniform, suggesting that the same editors were responsible for the whole work with the exception of these tractates. But even these tractates only differ slightly in style and vocabulary from the rest so that the impression is given of a co-ordinated editorial activity, though one carried out in at least two different places in Babylon. Although Palestinian Amoraim are frequently mentioned in the *Bavli* and Babylonian Amoraim in the *Yerushalmi* (naturally so since some of the Sages of each country visited the others from time to time, carrying the teachings with them), the weight of scholarly opinion is that the editors of the *Bavli* did not have before them the actual text of the *Yerushalmi*, nor did the Palestinian editors have anything like a proto-*Bavli*. If the editors of either had had reference to an actual text of the other, it is inconceivable that they would not have mentioned this. Here the argument from silence is very convincing.

The word Talmud also means 'Teaching' or 'Study' (from the root *limmed*, 'to learn') as does the Aramaic word Gemara, used, from the Middle Ages, as a synonym for Talmud. The material in the Talmud is of two kinds: Halakhah ('Law'), the legal material, embracing all the detailed rules and regulations of Jewish religious life in all its ramifications; and Aggadah (from the root *nagad*, 'to tell'), embracing all the non-legal topics, the theology, the history, the legends, the folk-tales and a host of other topics, anything, in fact, that is not *halakhic*. It has been estimated that the *halakhic* material comprises two-thirds of the whole work. This should not be taken to mean that there are clearly delineated sections, one of Halakhah,

3

the other of Aggadah. The editors, usually by association or similarity of theme, often introduce a piece of *aggadah* into an *halakhic* discussion and vice versa.

When speaking of the editors of the Talmud it is necessary to appreciate that the term is not used in the Talmud itself. Indeed, the Babylonian Talmud, in all its thirty and more folio volumes (in most editions), appears as if it dropped down from Heaven intact with not the slightest indication of how and by whom this gigantic compilation was put together. Yet it is clear beyond doubt that the words of the Tannaim and Amoraim mentioned in the *Bavli* appear in an editorial framework. The anonymous teachers — the Stammaim ('Anonymous Ones'), in David Halivni's phrase — are present everywhere, and it is the contention of this book that these unknown men are the real authors of the Talmud in the form we now have it, not, as it was and still is often thought, that they simply provided some additions to the work of the Amoraim.

The Babylonian Talmud in all current editions consists of the Mishnah, and the Gemara on each section of the Mishnah, that is, on each *mishnah* (the smallest section, as above) of the Mishnah as a whole. But properly speaking, the Talmud *Bavli* or the Gemara of the *Bavli* is the name given to the post-mishnaic material. (The Mishnah itself is, of course, a separate work compiled centuries before the *Bavli*.) There is a *Bavli* Talmud or Gemara to the Orders of *Mo'ed, Nashim, Nezikin* and *Kodashim* of the Mishnah, but none to *Zera'im* (except for tractate *Berakhot*) or to *Tohorot* (except for tractate *Niddah*). In the following table the names are given of the tractates on which there is a *Bavli*:

ZERA'IM
Berakhot

MO'ED
Shabbat, 'Eruvin, Pesaḥim, Yoma, Sukkah, Betzah, Rosh ha-Shanah, Ta'anit, Megillah, Mo'ed Katan, Ḥagigah

NASHIM
Yevamot, Ketubot, Nedarim, Nazir, Sotah, Gittin, Kiddushin

NEZIKIN
Bava Kama, Bava Metzia', Bava Batra, Sanhedrin, Makkot, Shevu'ot, 'Avodah Zarah, Horayot

KODASHIM
Zevaḥim, Menaḥot, Ḥullin, Bekhorot, 'Arakhin, Temurah, Keritot, Tamid

TOHOROT

Niddah

It is understandable why there is no *Bavli to Zera'im* since the agricultural laws only applied to the Holy Land. (There is, in fact, a *Yerushalmi* to *Zera'im*.) *Berakhot* is an exception because this tractate deals with prayer and benedictions, obviously applicable in Babylon as well. For a similar reason there is no *Bavli* (and no *Yerushalmi*) to *Tohorot*, with the exception of *Niddah* which deals with the separation of a wife from her husband during her menses and was hence of practical application even after the destruction of the Temple. It is something of a puzzle why, in that case, there is a *Bavli* (but no *Yerushalmi*) to *Kodashim*, the bulk of which was also inapplicable after the destruction of the Temple. The reason is probably because of the Rabbinic belief that to study the sacrificial system is accounted as if one had offered the sacrifices in the Temple. It has been argued that in the Middle Ages there did exist a *Yerushalmi* to *Kodashim*, which was later lost, but the evidence for this is totally inconclusive. (Parts of the 'lost' *Yerushalmi* to *Kodashim* appeared in print at the beginning of this century but this, it has now been established, is nothing more than a clever forgery.)

For further details the articles on the Talmud in the Jewish Encyclopaedia and the Encyclopaedia Judaica should be consulted, and the standard introductions by Albeck, Strack and Meilziner as given in the bibliography of this book.

The word *sugya* (pl. *sugyot*), used repeatedly in this book is the technical term for a Talmudic unit complete in itself, though it might also form part of a larger unit; that is to say, a Talmudic passage in which a particular topic is treated in full. Although based on Talmudic usage, the term in this sense is post-Talmudic. The Talmud nowhere gives any label to its units but, by early convention and throughout the history of Talmudic studies, the term *sugya* is used to denote such units.

1

How much of the Babylonian Talmud is pseudepigraphic?

Students of the Babylonian Talmud are aware that many of the statements attributed in the work to various teachers are not necessarily authentic. We are not here concerned with the question of the reliability of the transmission as much as with the phenomenon that some of the statements, at least, were never intended to be understood as the actual remarks of the teachers to whom they are attributed. In other words, some of them are pseudepigraphic. Pseudepigraphic Rabbinic statements are not limited, of course, to the Babylonian Talmud, but it will be argued that in this work the pseudepigraphic element is prevalent to a remarkable degree.

In the case of an acknowledged pseudepigraphic work like the Zohar, the problem can be seen clearly. No one nowadays would dream of quoting the numerous Zoharic statements put into the mouth of R. Simeon b. Yohai, R. Eleazar, R. Hamnuna Sava and the other heroes of the Zohar as those actually uttered by the second- to fourth-century teachers themselves. It is generally recognised that these sayings were never intended to be accurate reportage, and that while they tell us a great deal about late thirteenth-century Spanish Jewish thought, they tell us nothing at all about Jewish thought in the second- to fourth-century Palestine. R. Simeon b. Yohai in the Zohar serves in exactly the same role as Bunyan's Pilgrim in *Pilgrim's Progress.*

Now it would be the height of absurdity to see the whole of the Babylonian Talmud as pseudepigraphic in this sense. The strongest circumstantial evidence tells against such a preposterous theory. Statements are attributed to teachers in such a way as to demonstrate beyond doubt that these teachers held consistent views which can be seen to have been occasioned by the particular conditions obtaining in a particular time. Moreover, sayings attributed to teachers in the Babylonian Talmud are frequently attributed to the same in the Jerusalem Talmud.

The question to be asked, therefore, is not whether the Babylonian Talmud as a whole is a pseudepigraphic work — it patently is not — but how much of the work is pseudepigraphic, and it is here contended that the answer to the question is, far more than is generally recognised. The evidence marshalled here is sufficient to show that there is so much pseudepigraphic material in the Babylonian Talmud that the greatest caution must be exercised by historians who use the Babylonian Talmud for the reconstruction of the lives of the Amoraim and the period in which they lived. It is to the credit of Professor J. Neusner and his school that our attention has been drawn to the need for caution in so much of this kind of reconstruction.[1] Our concern, however, is with the Amoraic period,[2] and with particular reference to the Babylonian Talmud. Scholars have noted some of the material to be presented but, so far as I am aware, this is the first attempt to summarise the material as a whole for the purpose of uncovering this important aspect of the Talmudic methodology.

We begin with a number of instances in which the Talmud itself explicitly acknowledges the pseudepigraphic nature of statements found therein.

Berakhot 27b

R. Zera said, R. Assi said, R. Eleazar said, R. Hanina said, Rav said: 'At the side of this pillar R. Ishmael son of R. Jose recited the *tefillah* of the Sabbath on the eve of the Sabbath.' When Ulla came, he said: 'It was at the side of a palm tree and not at the side of a pillar; and it was not R. Ishmael son of R. Jose but R. Eleazar son of R. Jose; and it was not the *tefillah* of the Sabbath on the eve of the Sabbath but the *tefillah* of the termination of the Sabbath on the Sabbath.'[3]

This passage is quite different from the more usual Talmudic passages containing two versions of a saying or episode. No less than five Amoraim are reported as making the original statement (or rather, one quoting the saying of the other until Rav's saying is reproduced) and yet Ulla is then cited as contradicting the original report in such a way as to make it appear wrong in every particular. The literary style of the passage should especially be noted. The editors have not been content with reporting two different versions of what is alleged to have taken place. Instead they first give it as 'R. Zera *said*, R. Assi *said*, etc.,' and only afterwards, in the name of

Ulla, do they turn the whole thing on its head. It is obvious that when the editors came to record this passage, they knew that it was at least doubtful whether, in fact, R. Zera really *said* it or R. Assi and others really *said* it, and yet they still see fit to use the word 'said' even though they go on immediately to contradict the 'saying' in the name of Ulla. Thus 'R. Zera (etc.) *said* ' does not mean that there is a reliable tradition that he actually did say it, only that the saying is attributed to him. It is not beyond the bounds of possibility that this whole passage may be a kind of skit on the dangers of inaccurate reporting, as if to say, here are five teachers in whose name something is reported in the most circumstantial detail, and yet the report is wrong in every respect: a 'pillar' being substituted for a 'palm tree'; R. Ishmael son of R. Jose for R. Eleazar son of R. Jose; and one type of Sabbath prayer for another. In any event, we have an instance of the editors recording 'R. Zera (etc.) *said*' when they take no pains to hide that they are far from certain that he really did say it.

'Avodah Zara 22a[4]

There were saffron-growers: the Gentile looking after the field on the Sabbath and the Israelite on the first day of the week. When they came before Rava, he permitted the arrangement. Ravina raised an objection to Rava's ruling: 'If an Israelite and a Gentile leased a field in partnership, the Israelite must not say to the Gentile: "Take your portion for the Sabbath work and I shall take mine from the work done on the week-day." But if this condition were made at the beginning it is permitted. And it is forbidden if they made a calculation.'[5] Rava suffered embarrassment. It then became known that they had, in fact, made their condition at the beginning. R. Gaviha of Be-Katil said: 'That was a case of *'orlah* plants (Leviticus 19:23), where the Gentile ate during the *'orlah* years and the Israelite during the permitted years. They came before Rava and he permitted it. But did not Ravina raise an objection to Rava's ruling? It was, in fact, to support Rava's ruling.[6] But Rava was embarrassed? That never happened at all.

An astonishing passage! First it is stated that the case that came before Rava was a Sabbath case. Rava's ruling was in flat contradiction to the *baraita* quoted by Ravina, and Rava was embarrassed at having given a wrong ruling. Later on, it is said, it was discovered that Rava's ruling was correct because the two had made a stipulation to the effect from the beginning. R. Gaviha then is reported as saying that the case was not a Sabbath case at all but a case concerning *'orlah*.

From the *baraita* it now emerges that this is permitted and it was in this connection that Rava gave his — correct — ruling. But then, it is asked, why did Ravina quote the *baraita* as a refutation of Rava? To this the reply is given that he did not, in fact, try to refute Rava from the *baraita* but, on the contrary, quoted the *baraita* in support of Rava. Why, then was Rava embarrassed? To this the reply is given that Rava was not embarrassed, i.e. that the original report was in error. Thus the editors are stating here quite explicitly that the whole apparently factual report of Ravina objecting to Rava's ruling and Rava suffering embarrassment as a result of it was pure fiction.[7]

What we have here, again, is far more than two different versions of a saying or episode. According to the report of R. Gaviha, which the editors have in fact recorded, the original episode and the debate and discussion around it never took place. And yet the editors still record it as if it took place.

Bava Batra 54a

Rav said, 'If one drew a picture on [the walls of] an estate of a proselyte [who has no heirs and whose property is consequently ownerless] he acquires it', for Rav only acquired the garden of the house of Rav by drawing a picture [on the walls].

Although the passage is prefaced by 'Rav said', in fact it goes on to say that Rav did not actually say it, but it is a ruling that can be inferred from Rav's own practice and hence it is as if Rav had actually said it.[8]

Bava Metzia' 70a

R. Anan said Samuel said: 'It is permitted to lend out orphans' money on interest.' R. Nahman said to him: 'Are we to feed them that which is forbidden simply because they are orphans? Orphans who eat that which is not theirs let them go after their testator.' He [R. Nahman] said to him [R. Anan]: 'Tell me what actually transpired?' He said: 'A cauldron belonging to the [orphaned] children of Mar Ukba was in the house of Mar Samuel and he weighed it before hiring it out, and he weighed it when it was returned, and he charged for its hire and for the loss of weight.' But if there was a fee for hiring there should have been no charge for loss of weight, and if there was a charge for loss of weight there should have been no charge for hiring. [Thus it was a case of Mar Samuel lending orphans' money on interest]. He [R. Nahman] said to him [R. Anan]: 'That would be permitted even if they were bearded men [adults]. For they stand the loss of wear and tear. For the more a copper is burnt the greater its depreciation.'

In this passage R. Anan states that Samuel *said*: 'It is permitted to lend out orphans' money on interest.' R. Nahman objects that Samuel cannot possibly have said this. It is forbidden to lend out orphans' money on interest. R. Nahman suggests that R. Anan could not have heard such a ruling from Samuel, but must have inferred it from some episode in which Samuel was involved. R. Anan then quotes the episode and agrees that it was from this that he inferred the ruling attributed to Samuel, not as a direct ruling from Samuel himself. To this R. Nahman retorts that R. Anan's inference was wrong since in the episode no question of interest was involved. Thus, although R. Anan is reported as saying that Samuel *said* it, in fact he did not mean that Samuel had actually *said* it, but he 'said it' by virtue of his practice in the case of the orphans and their cauldron.[9]

Shabbat 115a

If the Day of Atonement falls on the Sabbath, the trimming of vegetables is permitted. Nuts may be cracked and pomegranates scraped from the time of *minhah* onwards because of grief [i.e. it would cause grief to people if these had to be done after the long fast]. In the household of R. Judah they used to trim cabbage. In the household of Rabbah they used to scrape pumpkins. When he noticed that they were doing this too early [i.e. before the time of *minhah*], he said to them: 'A letter has come from the west in the name of R. Johanan stating that it is forbidden.'

The meaning of this passage would seem to be that there was no actual letter of R. Johanan since Rabbah did not disclose its existence until he saw that the members of his household were taking advantage of the dispensation by scraping the pumpkins too early. Evidently, there was no objection to inventing statements and attributing them to a famous authority if the motive was to increase respect for the law.[10]

'Eruvin 51a

Rabbah and R. Joseph were on a journey [on the eve of the Sabbath]. Rabbah said to R. Joseph: 'Let our Sabbath domicile be under the palm tree that supports another tree.' 'I do not know such a tree,' said he. 'Rely on me,' he replied. For it has been taught: R. Jose says: 'If there were two, and one knew of a place and the other did not, the one who does not know transfers his choice to one who does know who then declares: "Let our Sabbath domicile be in such-and-such a place".' But it was not so. He [Rabbah] only attributed it to R. Jose so that he [R. Joseph] would accept it since R. Jose has depths to his teachings [i.e. he is an acknowledged authority].

In this passage again it is stated explicitly that Rabbah did not really know of a ruling by R. Jose but invented it for the benefit of R. Joseph.[11]

Gittin 20a

It was taught: Rabbi says: 'If he wrote it [a bill of divorce] on something from which it is forbidden to derive any benefit it is still valid.' Levi went and expounded this ruling in the name of Rabbi and it was not praised. [He then stated it] in the name of many [*rabbim*, similar in sound to *rabbi*] and it was praised.

Levi held the ruling of Rabbi to be correct, but when he noticed that Rabbi's authority was insufficiently strong to convince others he stated it in the name of the 'many'. Possibly the meaning here is that the word *'rabbim'* is very similar to the word *'rabbi'* so that Levi only had to add the final *mem*. In any event it is clearly asserted that Levi had no compunction about attributing to the 'many' a ruling they never gave.[12]

Ḥullin 111b

It was said: If fish were placed in a [hot] dish: Rav said: 'It is forbidden to eat them with a milk sauce.' Samuel said: 'It is permitted to eat them with milk sauce . . .' R. Eleazar came before Samuel who was eating together with milk sauce fish that had been placed in a meat dish. He [Samuel] offered some to R. Eleazar who refused to eat. Said he [Samuel]: 'When I gave it to your master [Rav] he ate and you will not eat.' When he [R. Eleazar] came before Rav he said: 'Has the master gone back on his ruling?' He replied: 'God forbid that the son of Abba bar Abba [i.e. Samuel] should ever have given me to eat that which I hold to be forbidden.'

In this passage it is stated that Samuel invented the episode about Rav eating the fish in order to persuade R. Eleazar to eat it. When Rav is informed of this he denies that it ever happened.[13]

Pesaḥim 26b–27a

Our Rabbis taught: If an oven had been heated by means of the husks of *'orlah* or the stubble of mixed seeds in a vineyard: If it is new it must be demolished [because the forbidden stubble has fired it making it into an oven], but if it is old it must be allowed to cool [before baking in it]. If he baked bread in the oven: Rabbi says: 'The bread is forbidden.' But the Sages say: The bread is permitted . . .' R. Joseph said, R. Judah said, Samuel said: 'If an oven had been heated by means of the husks of *'orlah* or the stubble of mixed seeds in a vineyard: If it is new it must be demolished but if it is old it must be allowed to cool. If he baked bread in the oven: Rabbi says: 'The bread is permitted.' But the Sages say: 'The bread is forbidden.' But we have been taught the opposite [that it is Rabbi who forbids it and the Sages who permit it]? Samuel had it in the reverse order [i.e. in his version of the *baraita*, it was Rabbi who said the bread is permitted]. Or if you want I can say, Samuel held that the ruling follows the opinion of Rabbi where he debates the matter with only one of his colleagues, but not where the debate is with a number of his colleagues. Yet in this case Samuel held that the ruling follows the opinion of Rabbi, even though here the debate is with a number of his colleagues. Consequently, Samuel decided to teach the *baraita* in the reverse order [that it is the Sages who forbid it and Rabbi who permits] so that the opinion of the Sages should stand as being prohibitive.[14]

It is suggested, in the 'If you want I can say' version, that Samuel knew quite well that it was the Sages who said the bread was permitted and Rabbi that it was forbidden. But since Samuel held that, in fact, contrary to the usual procedure, the ruling here follows the opinion of Rabbi, he consciously reversed the names so that people would accept the view of Rabbi which he, Samuel, conveyed as if it were the opinion of the Sages.

From these latter instances it appears that while there is much concern in the Talmudic literature about giving the author of a saying his due by repeating it in his name,[15] this is not on grounds of accuracy but to do otherwise, to suggest that a teacher's saying was not of his own, is a form of theft.[16] What is condemned is plagiarism, but there seems to have been no objection at all to attributing sayings to teachers who were not actually responsible for them.[17]

So far we have noted some instances where there is an explicit statement that the matter is pseudepigraphic. In addition to these there are numerous instances where the pseudepigraphic nature of the material is beyond doubt even though this is not stated explicitly.

First to be considered are the numerous *aggadic* passages (not confined to the Babylonian Talmud) where words are put into the mouths of early teachers without the slightest suggestion that they actually uttered these words. Of course there are many instances where the editors of the Talmud do appear to be claiming that statements put into the mouths of earlier heroes are the authentic sayings of these teachers. But that the converse is also true can be seen from the fact that sayings are frequently attributed to Biblical heroes or legendary figures and these in exactly the same style as that used for reports about sayings of contemporaries or near contemporaries. Nahman Krochmal[18] demonstrated long ago that, for example, anachronistic statements are attributed to Biblical heroes and villains which they could not possibly have made; the concern of those who made the attribution being no more than the expression of some moral teaching that could best be conveyed by the construction of an imaginary dialogue or a fictitious episode around some Biblical character. Of this order are the sayings attributed to the disciples of Jesus as they were being taken out to be executed (*Sanhedrin* 42b), where the whole passage consists of puns on their names. Once this genre is recognised, it becomes impossible to believe that the teachers involved held themselves to be engaged in reportage. It is rather that they were consciously engaged in literary fiction, albeit with a moral or religious purpose. The same applies to the dialogue between R. Jose and Elijah (*Berakhot* 3a) and, for that matter, to all the other 'reports' of conversation between Elijah and a Rabbinic hero.[19] How much ink has been spilled on the 'saying' of Hillel (*Shabbat* 31a) to the prospective proselyte, without any appreciation that the three tales of Hillel and Shammai and the proselytes are intended chiefly to demonstrate the need for a teacher to have patience, as the preface to the tales has it: 'Let a man always be humble like Hillel and never quick-tempered like Shammai.'[20] Hillel and Shammai are the heroes of these tales but to imagine that they actually said what they are said to have said, or that this was the intention of the tellers of the tales, is akin to attempting to reconstruct that biography and teaching of, shall we say, Joseph or Abraham from the numerous *midrashic* and *aggadic* sayings regarding what these Biblical figures are reported to have said.[21] The reliability of reports in the Talmud about someone saying this or that is another extremely complicated question. The point to which attention is called here is that in the instances quoted, and in many others, there was no intention in the first instance of conveying a reliable report. To see otherwise is to ask what Mark Antony really meant when *he* said: 'Friends, Romans, countrymen, lend me your ears.'

Ketubot 9a

R. Eleazar said: 'If a man says: I found an "open door" [i.e. that his wife was not a virgin], he is believed to render her forbidden to him.'

A careful examination of the whole *sugya* here shows that R. Eleazar's concern is said to be whether the man is *believed*, the principle being that of a man rendering something forbidden for himself alone (*ḥatikhah de-issura*) where there is insufficient evidence for it to be forbidden by law.[22] But the Jerusalem Talmud[23] formulates it as: 'R. Illa said in the name of R. Eleazar: If he found an "open door" he is forbidden to keep her because she is a doubtful *sotah*.' Thus while both the Babylonian and Jerusalem Talmud report the saying of R. Eleazar, there is nothing in the Jerusalem Talmud about the man being 'believed.' When we appreciate that the whole *sugya* in the Babylonian Talmud is concerned with the question of whether the man is 'believed,' it follows, surely, that R. Eleazar was not known actually to have used the words 'he is believed,' etc, but it is rather a case of the Babylonian Talmud putting these words into R. Eleazar's mouth for the purpose of conducting the subsequent discussion. If this is correct, the words 'R. Eleazar said: "If a man says . . . he is *believed*" are not intended to convey R. Eleazar's *ipsissima verba*, but mean rather that from a reported ruling of R. Eleazar it can be concluded that this is what R. Eleazar is *saying*.

Horayot 13b

What shall we [R. Meir and R. Nathan] say to him [R. Simeon b. Gamaliel]? We will say to him: Reveal [i.e. expound] *'Uktzin* which he does not have [i.e. he is unfamiliar with it] and since he did not learn it we shall say to him, *Who can express the mighty acts of the Lord: make all His praises be heard* (Psalm 105:2); who is fit to declare the mighty acts of the Lord [i.e. to teach the Torah]? One who can make *all* His praises be heard. We shall then depose him and I shall become Av Bet Din and you the Nasi . . . On the following day they said to him: 'Let the Master expound *'Uktzin.*' He ordered them to be expelled from the Bet ha-Midrash. They wrote out difficulties on scraps of paper and threw these there. That which he [R. Simeon b. Gamaliel] was able to solve he solved, but of those he was unable to solve they themselves wrote down the solutions and

14

threw them in . . . R. Simeon b. Gamaliel said: 'We shall readmit them but impose this penalty that no statement (*shema'ata*) will ever be reported in their name.'

This is the account in the Babylonian Talmud of the controversy between Rabban Simeon b. Gamaliel and R. Meir and R. Nathan. Now practically every detail of the alleged conflict is taken from procedures among the Babylonian Amoraim, for example the term *shema'ata*;[24] the lack of familiarity with '*Uktzin*;[25] the saying about declaring God's praises;[26] and the practice of writing difficulties on scraps of paper.[27] In other words this is a Babylonian *tale* about events said to have taken place perhaps centuries before the tale was told.[28] It is one of the great puzzles of Talmudic historiography that sober scholars of renown should have used this material in trying to reconstruct what actually happened at the time of the controversy.[29]

The use of names in the Talmud

Of importance to our investigation is the peculiar phenomenon, found also in the Midrash, of attributing rulings and sayings to teachers whose name is a pun on the subject-matter of that particular saying,[30] as, for example, when R. Abba bar Memel explains the meaning of the term *memel* in the Mishnah.[31] The explanation of this phenomenon by Z. H. Chajes,[32] that it only applies to scholars not otherwise noted for their sayings so that the name was given to them because of the saying, cannot be substantiated, as R. Margaliot has pointed out.[33] Nor is Margaliot's own solution (that because of their names the scholars were attracted to sayings with a pun on these names)[34] anything but weak. Surely the most plausible explanation is that we have here a literary device in which the names of the scholars were appended to the sayings precisely because of the pun. If this is correct, it can only mean that the scholars did not say these things at all but it is all the work of the editors or, at least, part of the long editorial process.[35]

The application of an original saying

Another phenomenon for our investigation is that of the same scholar being quoted in a number of passages as *saying* this or that and quoted moreover in the identical words even though the contexts are different.[36] For instance, in three different passages[37] R. Jeremiah is quoted as asking whether a to-and-fro movement is to be counted as one or as two, and in a number of different contexts R. Pappa[38] is quoted as *saying*, 'Therefore we should say both of them.' Surely the best way of understanding this phenomenon is that R. Jeremiah and R. Pappa only *said* it once, in a particular context, it is the editors who supplied it to all other instances where it was suitable.[39] If this is correct, in all but the original instance the meaning is not that R. Jeremiah or R. Pappa actually said it where he is said to have *said* it, but rather that from the original saying it can be concluded that he would 'say' it here too and by 'saying' it there he, in fact, 'says' it here as well.[40]

In the light of our investigation it will be seen how extremely precarious it is to conclude, without further very careful examination, that when the Talmud reports a teacher as 'saying' something he actually did say it. And yet it is frightening to observe how many scholars are guilty of precisely this. We repeat, it is not only the question of reliability that is involved, though that too must not be brushed aside, but the wider question of whether some statements were ever intended to be recorded as authentic. We conclude with a number of examples, taken at random, of this lack of due caution through a failure to recognise the pseudepigraphic nature of the material.

H. Albeck, for instance,[41] in his account of Rabbah bar bar Hana is, as we might have expected, cautious in his use of the sources for historical reconstruction. For all that, he concludes his note with these words, 'Well-known are his [Rabbah bar bar Hana's] marvellous tales regarding his journeys on the sea and through the desert and his conversations with other travellers he met,' quoting as his source the famous passage in *Bava Batra* 73b. Albeck thus seems to take it for granted that when the Talmud in that passage tells us that Rabbah bar bar Hana *said* this or that, the intention is to convey an actual saying or tale of Rabbah bar bar Hana said or told himself. Rabbah bar bar Hana has been described as the 'Sinbad the Sailor' of the Talmud.[42] Exactly! And one should as little quote Rabbah bar bar Hana as the author of 'his' tales, as quote Sinbad as the author of 'his' tales in *The Arabian Nights*. Rabbah bar bar Hana is the hero of the tales 'he' tells, not their author.

Dealing with the life of R. Meir, A. Oppenheim remarks,[43] 'One tradition holds that his real name was R. Nehorai . . . but that he was

16

called Meir ["the illuminator"] because "he enlightened the eyes of the Sages," ' quoting as his source '*Eruvin* 13b. This passage can by no stretch of the imagination be termed a 'tradition' and is no more than a very late punning on names.[44] What we have in the passage is a homily on teaching and learning pegged on to the name of R. Meir.[45]

Describing the career of R. Akiba, H. Freedman remarks:[46] 'While much that is told of him is undoubtedly colored by legend, it is clear that in his early years he was not only unlearned, an '*am ha-aretz*, but also a bitter enemy of the scholars, as he himself relates: "When I was an '*am ha-aretz* I said: 'Had I a scholar in my power, I would maul him like an ass' " (quoting *Pesaḥim* 49b). But in the context the concern is not with R. Akiba at all, but with the nature of the '*am ha-aretz*.[47] In this context a number of tales are told for the purpose of illustrating the enmity between the ignorant and the scholars, and R. Akiba features as the hero of one of these tales. It is beyond belief that a scholar who does not fail to recognise the purely legendary nature of a good deal of R. Akiba's biography can still quote this passage and, basing himself on it, permit himself to say: 'As he himself relates.'

How much of the Babylonian Talmud is pseudepigraphic? Certainly not all of it; that would be a ridiculous notion. Some of it is, however, undoubtedly pseudepigraphic and far more than is commonly appreciated. The detection of a strong pseudepigraphic element in the Babylonian Talmud ought to encourage the serious student of the Talmud, whenever he comes across a saying or ruling attributed to Rabbi A or B, to ask not only did Rabbi A or B really say it, but does the Talmud mean us to conclude that he really said it or is it no more than a not unusual literary device.

2

The Babylonian Talmud:
an academic work

As Jewish law developed, the Babylonian Talmud came to be seen as the main source of the whole legal system and the final Court of Appeal, so to speak.[1] The Babylonian Talmud itself, at least in the *halakhic* portions of the work,[2] became a kind of law code, with its main thrust in the direction of practical *halakhic* decisions. Historically speaking, this view of the Talmud is incorrect. On the contrary, the central feature of this gigantic work consists of purely academic investigation into legal theory. There is, of course, *some* practical *halakhic* material in the Talmud. There are, for example, many instances of case-law and of practical decisions. These practical aspects are, however, incidental to the theoretical. It is the argument itself that matters most, both to the Amoraim themselves and to the editors.[3]

First, it should be noted, that the Mishnah, to which the *Bavli* is appended, is largely theoretical in its thrust.[4] All the *mishnayot* dealing with the sacrificial system — the whole of *Seder Kodashim*, with the exception of *Ḥullin*; the first seven chapters of *Yoma*; chapters 5 through to 9 of *Pesaḥim*; *Shekalim*; *Ḥagigah*; parts of *Rosh ha-Shanah* and *Sukkah* — can only have been academic, since the Temple had long been destroyed at the time when the Mishnah was edited.[5] This applies also to the discussions regarding the obligation to bring a sin-offering, even in the 'practical' tractate of *Shabbat*.[6] Similarly, the major portion of *Sanhedrin* and the second chapter of *Makkot*, dealing as they do with capital punishment and exile to the cities of refuge, must be academic since capital punishment had long been in disuse when the Mishnah was edited.[7] Much of *Seder Toharot*, too, deals with topics that were of practical concern only in Temple times.[8]

Even in the *mishnayot* of *Zera'im* (of little practical consequence, incidentally, for the Babylonian Amoraim),[9] *Mo'ed*, *Nashim* and *Nezikin*, many of the topics discussed are obviously theoretical, for example, the references to complicated marriage relationships in *Yevamot;*[10] to the *androginos;*[11] to confusions in the Nazirite vows;[12] to the piling on of prohibitions for which there is the penalty of *malkut;*[13] to the *sotah;*[14] to some forms of the *get;*[15] to unlikely cases of the goring of oxen.[16] Thus the raw material upon which the Amoraim worked was very strong in its academic thrust. Moreover, all the *explanations* of the Mishnah in the *Bavli* are, as *mishnaic* exegesis, of an academic nature; the main aim is to understand the Mishnah rather than to apply its teachings.

The Amoraim studied the theoretical portions of the Mishnah with no less assiduity than the practical, as witness the existence in the *Bavli* of the Order of *Kodashim*. When R. Joseph objects to a statement that the *halakhah* is such and such in a matter having to do with capital punishment, 'A rule for the Messianic Age!' (i.e. it is of no practical consequence), Abaye retorts: 'In that case why study the Order of *Kodashim*? But it is a matter of study and will be rewarded as such' (i.e. the purely theoretical study of the Torah is of high value). R. Joseph agrees, holding that his objection was only to a statement of *halakhah*, i.e. of practical decision, when, in the nature of the case, there can be no decision until the Messianic Age.[17]

It is not only with regard to the study of the sacrificial system that the academic element is so prominent. This element appears constantly in the Babylonian Talmud whatever the subject-matter of the discussion, be it practical or theoretical. Whole types of material in the *Bavli* can have no other significance than that of purely academic exercises. The most ubiquitous of these is the *ba'ya*.

The Talmudic *ba'ya* consists of an academic problem regarding definition. The form is: a given statement can be understood either as X or as Y. Which is the correct definition? In M. Guttmann's well-known study of the *ba'ya*[18] with the title, '*Academic* problems in the Talmud' (*italics* mine), more than 1,200 of these are listed scattered throughout the Babylonian Talmud. The majority of these are extremely far-fetched. Very few of them, indeed, can ever have been presented as calling for a practical ruling. Since in every instance of the *ba'ya* the two halves are equally balanced, there is no reason for preferring X to Y. Indeed, in many instances the formula '*Teyku*' ('let it stand', 'leave it alone', 'it remains insoluble') is appended.[19] In other instances an attempt is made to solve the problem, but never by reasoning, only by quoting an authority who has come down either on the side of X or of Y. This means, in so many words, that there is no *reason* for preferring X to Y or Y to X, but it just so happens that the authority quoted, by favouring X or Y, has provided us with the correct definition. Guttmann compares the *ba'ya* with the problems set in pure mathematics, or with philosophical problems such as Zeno's dilemma of how Achilles can overtake the tortoise.

Another type of purely academic material in the *Bavli* consists of a list of different rules concerning a particular topic which, though the issue is one of practical *halakhah*, is so far-fetched that it is extremely unlikely that it will ever be presented to an authority for an actual ruling. The thrust in these instances is skilfully to compare the various rules to other known rules dealing with totally different matters from which, nonetheless, *halakhah* principles can be established.[20]

Another type of academic material is found in the first chapter of tractate *Kiddushin*,[21] where a series of artificial *kalin ve-ḥamurin* (arguments from the minor to the major) are presented and then refuted; the argument, for instance, that a married woman can obtain a release from her husband through the rite of *ḥalitzah* applicable to release from the levirate bond. Obviously, no one had ever thought that such was even a remote possibility.

The academic nature of much of the *Bavli* is not only to be perceived when the subjects discussed are of a purely academic nature. Even when the subject-matter is severely practical,[22] the discussion is often conducted in an academic way, almost as if the practical conclusion is of little interest apart from the stages in the argument by which it is reached. This is evident to every student of the Talmud, but as an illustration we note the first and longest (in number of words) tractate, *Berakhot*. There could hardly be more 'practical' topics than those treated in this tractate: — the reading of the *shema*; prayer; benedictions — all belonging to the daily life of the religious Jew. Yet, it is astonishing to observe, the bulk of the tractate is taken up with matters having only a very indirect relevance to practice, as the following analysis of the contents of the tractate demonstrates.

Berakhot, chapter 1, 2a–13a

The opening passage is in all probability a post-Talmudic addition.[23] It is, as in other opening passages, a literary investigation of the Mishnah with no practical consequences whatever. The next passage is similarly a comparison of the views of different Tannaim regarding the correct time for reading the evening *shema*. Interestingly enough, for our purpose, the practical rule, depending on which authority is followed, is not mentioned at all.[24] The discussion (3a) on how many 'watches' there are in the night has no practical significance.[25] There follows the *baraita* containing the story of Elijah and R. Jose, and another *baraita* stating the three reasons why one must not enter a ruin. The discussion (3a–b) on why three reasons are required does have practical consequences but, again, the main aim seems to be the elucidation of the *baraita*.

There follows a further discussion of the watches in the night, in which there is a saying by R. Zereka in the name of R. Ammi in the name of R. Joshua b. Levi and, in the usual pattern of the Talmud, there follows another saying in the name of these teachers. There then follows (3b–4a) a lengthy *aggadic* passage about David and Moses, which, like most *aggadic* passages, points to moral and religious lessons, but that is purely incidental. The discussion (4a–b) on the views of the Sages that the *shema* can only be read until midnight does have some practical rules, but these are not introduced as having importance in themselves but only as arising out of the discussion. There follows (4b) two disparate sayings of R. Eleazar bar Avina and the discussions on these.

The subject of the bedtime *shema* is now introduced and discussed briefly (4b–5a), after which there are sayings by R. Levi b. Hama in the name of R. Simeon b. Lakish and this leads into the topic of sufferings (5a–b). This is neither a practical nor even a precise theological statement, but consists rather of the use of theological material for a typical construction of the Talmudic *sugya*.[26]

There follows a list of sayings, in the form of *baraitot*, of Abba Benjamin and the discussion on these (5b–6a). One of these is on demons which leads to a discussion on demons which, in turn, leads to a lengthy *aggadic* passage (6a–8a). This passage contains a large number of different themes, including a very few of some practical consequence. The discussion on the views of Rabban Gamaliel (8b–9a), on the other hand, is of real practical consequence. The discussion that follows this (9a) on the correct time for eating the Paschal lamb obviously has no practical significance and the same applies to the *aggadic* passage which follows it (9a–b).

The opening discussion on the second *mishnah* (9b) has some practical import, but this is followed by another lengthy *aggadic* passage

(9b–10b) containing theoretical material into which a few practical rules have been inserted. The final comments to this *mishnah* (10b) are, however, of a practical nature.

The comments on the third *mishnah* (11a) are also practical, though here, too, the main interest appears to be in the casuistic discussion itself. The comments on the fourth *mishnah* (11a–12b) are the most practical of all we have so far considered, but even here purely academic argumentation is certainly not absent.[27] The comments on the final *mishnah* of this chapter (12b–13a) contain only one practical matter, that it is wrong to call the patriarchs by their early Scriptural names.

Berakhot, chapter 2, 13a–17b

The comments and discussion on the first *mishnah* (13a–15a) are, in the main, of practical significance, as are those on the second *mishnah* (15a–16a) and those on the third (16a–b). The comments on the final *mishnah* (16b–17b) consist first of a discussion on mourning for slaves (mentioned in the *mishnah*), followed by a list of prayers and maxims of various teachers and a discussion on these and, finally, a casuistic discussion of Rabban Simeon b. Gamaliel's views, referred to in the *mishnah*, all of which can only be said to be of practical consequence in a very loose sense.

Berakhot, chapter 3, 17b–26a

First there is a discussion on the laws regarding one whose near relative has died, mentioned in the *mishnah*. This leads to the well-known discussion on whether the dead know what transpires on earth (18a–19a) and contains a number of ghost-stories and a discussion of a ban imposed on scholars, the whole presented in the contrived manner typical of the Talmudic *sugya*.[28] There follows a further discussion on the *mishnah* (19a–b). Following on these is the *sugya* on respect for persons where a religious law is at stake (19b–20a), and an addition on the subject of miracles and another one on the evil eye (20a). Although the initial topic is a practical one, the theme is developed in the form of argument and counter-argument, thus making the thrust academic rather than practical.[29] The comment on the second *mishnah* (20b) is concerned with the practical question of the religious obligations of women, but is again casuistic and in the form of a single comment to the *mishnah*, concluding with the *aggadah* discussing why God shows favouritism to Israel (20b).

The lengthy comment on the third *mishnah* (20b–26a) is chiefly concerned with the practical questions of studying the Torah or praying where the person or place is unclean. But once again we see that the discussions are conducted in the academic vein typical of the Talmud, albeit with a predominance of practical *halakhah*.[30] The comment on the final *mishnah* (26a) is entirely academic.

Berakhot, chapter 4, 26a–30b

The comment on the first *mishnah* (26a–27b) deals with the practical question, discussed in the *mishnah*, of the times of the statutory daily prayers and other matters regarding prayer. The discussion proceeds by the typical casuistic method. There follows (27b–28a) the story of the deposition of Rabban Gamaliel II, hardly of any practical consequence for the Jews of Babylon in the Amoraic period. The final comments on this *mishnah* (28a–b) revert to the practical details of prayer. The second *mishnah* records only the prayer of R. Nehuniah b. Hakanah and the comment on it (28b) is similarly *aggadic* and purely theoretical, except for the form of prayer when entering and leaving the House of Study and this is, in fact, a quote from a *baraita*. The comments on the third *mishnah* (28b–30a) are in the form of both academic and practical discussion, as are the comments on the final *mishnah* (30a–b).

Berakhot, chapter 5, 30b–34d

The *mishnayot* in this chapter deal with questions of prayer, with the idea of preparations for prayer and forms of illegitimate types of prayer. The comments on the first *mishnah* (30b–33a) are a blend of the academic and the practical, the major portion of which is academic. The comments on the second *mishnah* (33a–b) are, like the *mishnah* itself, of a practical nature. The third *mishnah* and the comments (33b) are chiefly academic and deal with the illegitimate types of prayer and kindred topics. The comments on the fourth *mishnah* (34a–b) are mainly of practical significance. The final *mishnah* is of an *aggadic* nature, dealing with the theme of an error in prayer as a bad omen illustrated by the prayers of the miracle-working saint, R. Hanina b. Dosa. The comments (34b) are of the

the same nature, except for one or two rules at the end regarding the place of prayer.

Berakhot, chapter 6, 35a–46a

This chapter deals with the benedictions to be recited over various kinds of food and drink. The comments are similarly of practical consequence.

Berakhot, chapter 7, 45a–51b

This chapter, too, is practical, dealing with the laws of grace after meals and the comments follow the *mishnah.*

Berakhot, chapter 8, 51b–53b

The *mishnah* records the differences between the views of the House of Hillel and the House of Shammai regarding procedures at meals. The comments have the same practical aim.

Berakhot, chapter 9, 54a–64a

The *mishnah* deals with various forms of benedictions and prayers, concluding with a *midrash* on the *shema* and a statement regarding the Sadducean rejection of the doctrine of the World to Come. The comments are almost entirely *aggadic* with only a few practical matters considered.[31]

The interested reader is invited to examine other tractates of the Babylonian Talmud in order to discover how much of the material is academic. The thesis presented in this chapter is that far more academic material is found in the *Bavli* than is generally supposed. Here are three *sugyot*, taken at random, in support of the thesis.

Rosh ha-Shanah 28a

The *sugya* begins with the statement of the third-century Babylonian Amora, R. Judah, concerning one who used the horn of an animal, dedicated to the Temple as a sacrifice, as a *shofar*. Has he fulfilled his duty on the festival of *Rosh ha-Shanah* when the *shofar* has to be blown and heard. R. Judah observes that it depends on whether the animal had been set aside as a burnt-offering or as a peace-offering. To make use of an animal set aside as a burnt-offering, which has a higher degree of sanctity than a peace-offering, is to commit a trespass by virtue of which that which has been so used loses its sanctity. Consequently, R. Judah is made to argue,[32] if the *shofar* is from a burnt-offering, a trespass is committed by the very act of blowing. The horn thus loses its sanctity and so no sacred object has been used. One who has blown such a *shofar* has, therefore, fulfilled his obligation. It is otherwise with regard to the peace-offering. Since this has a lesser degree of sanctity, there is no law of trespass to make it lose its sanctity. Hence the one who has blown such a *shofar* has not fulfilled his obligation.

Rava (fourth century) objects that the trespass by means of which the horn loses its sanctity is the actual blowing. The horn only loses its sanctity afterwards. Why, then, does R. Judah state that the blower has fulfilled his obligation? Consequently, Rava disagrees with R. Judah, holding that in both cases the blower has not fulfilled his obligation. Later on, however, Rava changes his mind, holding that in both cases he has fulfilled his obligation. This is because the use of the horn to fulfil the precept of blowing the *shofar* does not constitute *profane* use and is permitted. Hence he has fulfilled his obligation.

Another statement of R. Judah is now recorded. The horn of an animal set aside for use as a sacrifice to idols should not, in the first instance, be used as a *shofar*, but if it had been so used the obligation has been fulfilled. But if the horn belongs to a devoted city (Deuteronomy 13: 11–17), he has not fulfilled his obligation since it is seen as pulverised, i.e. since everything that is in the city has to be burned, it is considered as if it has already been reduced to ashes so that there is no whole *shofar*, only bits of *shofar* matter, and the use of a whole *shofar* is required for the precept to be carried out.

Another statement of Rava now follows. If a man had made a vow to enjoy no benefit from a *shofar* he may still use it as a *shofar* on *Rosh ha-Shanah*, since (as in Rava's first statement) the use of something from which it is forbidden to have benefit does not apply when it is used in order to fulfil a religious duty. That is not called a 'benefit' within the limits of that term. For the same reason, Rava holds that if A takes a vow to have no benefit from B, B may nonetheless sprinkle upon A the ashes of the red heifer in order to effect A's purification (Numbers 19). But this is only permitted in winter. In summer the sprinkling of the ashes mingled with water would have a welcome cooling effect and that would constitute a 'benefit', even though the actual purification rite does not.

This is an excellent illustration of the purely academic thrust of the Babylonian Talmud. While subtle theories are debated and subtle legal distinctions made, it all has no reference whatsoever (directly at least) to any practical question regarding its main theme, the sounding of the *shofar* on *Rosh ha-Shanah*. The Temple had been destroyed long before so that, when the discussions were recorded, there was no such thing as a *shofar* of a burnt-offering or a peace-offering and no sprinkling water of purification.[33] There was no 'devoted city', and it is extremely far-fetched to imagine that R. Judah was concerned with any actual case of a Babylonian Jew who wished to use a *shofar* taken from an animal set aside for idolatrous purposes. Clearly, the material used for the subtle distinctions is irrelevant as long as it could provide the bricks for the construction of the edifice that is the *sugya*. And it is our contention that the same applies to the bulk of the Babylonian Talmud.

Kiddushin 51a–52a

This *sugya* contains the famous debate between Abbaye and Rava concerning 'betrothal that cannot lead to intercourse' (*kiddushin she-eyn mesurin le-viah*). The case is where a man betroths one of two sisters without specifying which one, i.e. he delivers the betrothal money to someone acting on behalf of both sisters but declares, 'One of you be betrothed unto me with this money,' without specifying which of the sisters he wishes to betroth. He cannot have intercourse with either of the women since she may be his wife's sister. Rava argues that such a betrothal, which is bound to frustrate the very purpose of marriage, is not a valid betrothal at all so that each of the two sisters can marry another without having first to obtain a divorce from the man who sought to betroth one of them in this way. Abbaye disagrees with Rava. According to Abbaye, the betrothal is valid in the sense that neither of the two sisters can marry another without first obtaining a divorce. With great subtlety the Talmud argues the case, eventually coming down on the side of Abbaye.[34] Now is it at all likely that, in real life, a man would betroth one of two sisters in this way (where he gave them the choice it would be valid, and that is not the case considered by Abbaye and Rava)? And in the extremely unlikely event that someone did, would the case be of such significance to the Amoraim that they had to arrive at an immediate decision? But if the whole *sugya* is purely academic, it constitutes an intellectual exercise of much subtlety, justifiable on these grounds even if the actual case will never come before the Rabbis for a ruling.

Shabbat 5a–b

The principle laid down for the prohibition of carrying on the Sabbath from the private to the public domain or *vice versa*, or for carrying four cubits in the public domain, is that for there to be liability (of capital punishment where it is done intentionally and for a sin-offering where it is done unintentionally), the act must consist of two separate acts. There must be first a lifting-up of the object to be carried — *'akirah* — and, after the object thus lifted has been carried, the setting down of the object — *hanahah*. The Palestinian Amora, R. Johanan (third century) observes that if A threw an object (throwing counts as carrying) into the hands of B, who remains stationary, A is liable since he has performed the act with both *'akirah* and *hanahah*. But if B moved towards the object to catch it, A is not liable since A performed only the *'akirah*, the *hanahah* having been performed by B's action. (There is no liability for Sabbath acts performed by more than one person.) R. Johanan then sets this problem. What if A threw the object and then he himself ran to catch it? Is this considered as two half-acts — since if B had moved to catch the object, there is no liability — or, since after all it is A who carried out both the *'akirah* and the *hanahah*, A is liable?

Rava observes that if A took some water in his hand, carried it out and then placed it on water that is already there, A is liable. The placing of water on water constitutes *hanahah*. But if A placed a nut on water he is not liable. Here there is no real *hanahah* since the nut does not 'rest' on the water. What is the law, asks Rava, if A placed the nut in a vessel resting on the water? Relative to the vessel the nut 'rests,' but in relation to the water the nut does not 'rest.'

What could be more academic and theoretical than this discussion? It is not only that in the period of the Amoraim the question of liability, whether for capital punishment or for a sin-offering, could not have arisen. Even in Temple times, these problems can hardly have been of sufficient consequence to warrant a discussion on the *practical* ruling. Is it at all likely that such remote cases could ever have come before the courts for a decision? It is as clear as can be that what we have here, and in the numerous cases of a similar nature even in the 'practical' tractate *Shabbat*, is a series of purely academic exercises for the purpose of discussing the legal principles, even though there are no practical consequences, or rather, the discussions themselves are the practical consequences involved in the study of the Torah. The theoretical study of the Torah is itself the *practice* of a religious obligation of great value.[35]

On the face of it, there stands against the thesis of this chapter the traditional view that the ideal method of studying the Torah is for the debates and discussions to lead up to the rule in practice.[36] But this does not mean that the *sole* purpose of the discussions is to lead to practical conclusions, only that where the issue is of a practical nature there is a need to argue correctly so that the conclusion is in conformity with the actual law. In one of the three passages in which the ideal is mentioned,[37] it is applied specifically to one who is called upon to render decisions in Jewish law, i.e. if a scholar is called upon to render decisions he should get them right. In one of the other passages,[38] moreover, it is said that Moses prayed that Judah should be able to attain to the ideal in his discussions with the 'Rabbis' in Paradise. In other words, to get it right, to let the conclusions reached be correct, does not mean that only those laws which have practical application are worth studying. The Torah debates take place in Paradise — in the Yeshivah on High — where there are no practical consequences for earthly life.[39]

Our concern in this chapter has been with the *Bavli*. What of the *Yerushalmi*? It is possible that the Palestinian Amoraim and the final editors of the *Yerushalmi* were, indeed, more interested in practical law. Witness to this is perhaps the absence from the *Yerushalmi* of the lengthy type of discussion and argument so typical of the *Bavli* and the fact that there is a *Yerushalmi*, but no *Bavli*, to the Order *Zera'im*, the subject-matter of which was practical in Palestine but not in Babylon. In can be argued, too, that this is the reason for the absence of a *Yerushalmi* to the Order *Kodashim* (if, indeed, there ever was such an absence, a subject much debated in modern research). Yet, after all, a major part of the *Yerushalmi* too is in the form of *mishnaic* exegesis and thus a theoretical exercise. Moreover, in the *Yerushalmi*, as in the *Bavli*, there is an abundance of purely academic material, that is to say, discussions on topics for which it is extremely unlikely that Rabbis would ever be called upon to render actual decisions.

One need go no further than the very beginning of tractate *Berakhot* in the *Yerushalmi* to see that this is so. After stating that when three stars are seen in the night sky it is certainly night for the purposes of the law, whereas when only two stars can be seen it is doubtful whether it is night or day, the *Yerushalmi* proceeds to state the following.[40] If a man saw two stars on the eve of the Sabbath and he did some 'work' forbidden on the Sabbath and he again did some 'work' at the termination of the Sabbath when only two stars were seen, he is liable whichever way one looks at the matter. For if the two stars denote that it is still day, he is liable for the work he did at the termination of the Sabbath. But if the two stars denote that it is night, it follows that he is liable for the work he did on the eve of the Sabbath. As noted above, there was no liability for capital punishment or for a sin-offering in the Amoraic period and the issue is, in any event, so remote (doing work in the presence of witnesses when two and only two stars had been seen both on the eve of the Sabbath and at its termination) that the discussion cannot possibly have been of practical consequence. But as an illustration of the legal principles governing doubt in law in general and the doubt occasioned by the twilight period in particular, the discussion is an important, albeit theoretical, exercise.

To sum up. The editors of the Babylonian Talmud and, apparently, the Amoraim whose discussions feature in the work, saw no need to defend their emphasis on theory. The old Cambridge toast 'To pure Mathematics. May it never have any practical consequences whatever,' cannot to be sure, be applied to Talmudic theory. The Talmud is the basis of all subsequent Jewish law and study divorced from practice was, for the Rabbis, a vain pursuit. Yet, for them, the study of the Torah was in itself the highest form of worship and as such to be engaged in for its own sake, irrespective of whether the subject discussed was severely practical or purely theoretical. If the contention of this chapter is correct, it means that the Talmud is largely a work of pure theory. The academic nature of the Talmud did, indeed, present severe problems to the Codifiers, who were obliged to use as the source of their legislation a work with a very

29

different aim, at least in its major parts. In a kind of compensation, it was the academic aspect of the Talmud that inspired all subsequent generations of scholars, from the Tosafists to the *Ketzot ha-Ḥoshen*,[41] from Maimonides to the Ragadshover Gaon,[42] to tread the same path, devoting the major portion of their lives to theorising in Torah as a sublime religious activity, demanding and receiving total application of mind and heart.

3

Rabbinic views on the order and authorship of the Biblical books

This chapter seeks to examine afresh the passage in the Babylonian Talmud, *Bava Batra* 14b–15a, the *locus classicus* for Rabbinic views on the order and authorship of the Biblical books, referred to as such in the standard Introductions to the Old Testament; usually, it must be said, without any real understanding either of the passage itself or of the nature of the Talmudic literature in general. Among modern introductory works in which reference is made to this passage are W. Robertson Smith, *The Old Testament in the Jewish Church*;[1] S. R. Driver, *An Introduction to the Literature of the Old Testament*;[2] R. H. Pfeiffer, *Introduction to the Old Testament*;[3] A. Bentzen, *Introduction to the Old Testament*;[4] O. Eissfeldt, *The Old Testament An Introduction*;[5] and *Peake's Commentary to the Bible*.[6] In these and similar works the passage is quoted as the views of 'the Rabbis', with little attempt at considering questions of dating or how typical the passage is of Rabbinic opinion or whether, indeed, the passage forms a unit or is a composite work.

Before looking at the passage in detail, one or two observations are in order regarding its place in the Talmudic literature. Tractate *Bava Batra* deals with jurisprudential topics — conveyancing, inheritance, and the like — and seems, at first glance, to be the last place in which to expect a discussion on the Biblical books. The reason why the passage appears where it does is, following the usual pattern of Talmudic material, by association. The preceding section of the tractate considers the case of joint-owners of an article who wish to divide it — a typical '*Bava Batra*' theme. How is the division to be effected, and what if only one of the joint-owners wishes to divide or give the other the option of buying him out? In this context it is ruled that if the two have joint-ownership of a book of the Bible it must not be divided, i.e. cut in two, even if both agree to the division, since the sanctity of a Biblical book requires that it be left intact. This leads, purely by association, to the discussion on the order and authorship of the Biblical books.

Surprisingly, the passage is unique in that it is the only full-scale treatment of the question in the whole of the Rabbinic literature; though, naturally, there are brief discussions elsewhere in the literature on aspects of authorship of this or that Biblical book. Nowhere else do we find any discussion of the 'order' of the Biblical books.

Both the incidental, casual manner in which the topic is introduced and the absence of any parallel passage elsewhere cry out for explanation. One would have thought the Rabbis to be more profoundly interested in who wrote the Biblical books than to devote to the question no more than a single passage in the whole, vast literature and to introduce even that passage in an off-hand manner, so to speak. The truth is, as all the indications go to show, that the Rabbis were *not* particularly interested in who wrote the Biblical books. What mattered to them was that the books were inspired, albeit with varying degrees of inspiration. The question of who actually recorded the inspired words in writing was quite secondary, of neither greater nor lesser interest than other historical questions with no implications for the practical life of religion.

To turn to the passage itself, this consists of two parts. The core of the passage is a *baraita*, a Tannaitic source compiled not later than the end of the second century CE. The other part consists of the comments on the *baraita* by the anonymous editors of the Talmud. This editorial material, the main subject of the inquiry in this book, dates probably from as late as the end of the fifth century CE.[7] From the Middle Ages, it should be noted, perceptive students of the Talmud have recognised — this is axiomatic for modern scholars — that the framework material provided by the anonymous editors is not necessarily an accurate exposition of the Tannaitic material, so that scholars who lump together both sets of material, divided by several centuries, the one in Palestine, the other in Babylon, are way off the mark. It has already been noted that the final editors exercised considerable freedom in the use of earlier material for their own purposes. This whole question will receive detailed treatment in the following chapters. This chapter takes up the theme. The investigation of the *Bava Batra* passage is relevant to the inquiry in another way as well in that, in noting how the Rabbis thought the Biblical books were compiled and arranged, fresh light is thrown on how the Rabbinic literature, especially the Babylonian

Talmud, was compiled and arranged. The statements of the Rabbis on the compilation of the Biblical books seem to reflect the conditions under which their own books were compiled.

The Talmudic source

The baraita, introduced with the usual formula *teno rabbanan*, 'Our Rabbis taught,' reads:

The Order of the Prophets: Joshua and Judges; Samuel and Kings; Jeremiah and Ezekiel; Isaiah and The Twelve. The order of the *Ketuvim* [the Hagiographa]: Ruth; the Book of Psalms; Job; Proverbs; Ecclesiastes; Song of Songs; Lamentations; Daniel; the Scroll of Esther; Ezra and Chronicles. And who wrote them? Moses wrote his book; the portion of Balaam and Job. Joshua wrote his book and the last eight verses of the Torah. Samuel wrote his book, Judges and Ruth. David wrote the Book of Psalms through (*'al yedey*) ten elders, namely, Adam, Melchizedek, Abraham, Moses, Heman, Yeduthun, Asaph and the three sons of Korah. Jeremiah wrote his book, the Book of Kings and Lamentations. Hezekiah and his associates wrote Isaiah, Proverbs, Song of Songs and Ecclesiastes. The Men of the Great Synagogue wrote Ezekiel, The Twelve, Daniel and the Scroll of Esther. Ezra wrote his book and the genealogies to his own.

It can be seen that the *baraita* is in three sections (or, possibly, there are three separate *baraitot*).[8] There is first, the statement about the order of the Prophets. Secondly, there is the statement about the order of the *Ketuvim*. Finally, there is the statement about authorship of the books.

What precisely is the meaning of the 'order' (*sidran*) of the Prophets. Nahum Sarna, in his essay, 'The Order of the Books,'[9] has argued that it cannot mean the order in which the books are to be written in a single scroll since each book was, in fact, written separately. Nor can it mean that the books were to be written in this order in a codex since the Jews did not use codex form until centuries later. Sarna's ingenious suggestion is that 'order' here refers to the arrangement of the books on the shelves of the libraries in which they were kept, and lists of these drawn up to facilitate reference. Although Sarna adduces some evidence of this method of storing in the Hellenistic world, there is no reference to Jews using this method, or indeed to libraries of books, in Tannaitic times. It is possible that, *contra* Sarna, the 'order' of the *baraita* does refer to the order in which the books have to be written in a single scroll.

While it is true that it was unusual for more than one book to be written in a single scroll, it is clear from the Talmudic discussion immediately preceding our passage that more than one book was occasionally written on a single scroll. This is the meaning of 'joining' (*medubbakim*) in the previous passage.[10]

It is astonishing to me that neither the classical commentators to *Bava Batra*, nor the modern scholars who have commented on our passage, have noticed that since the various books are listed in the *baraita* in chronological order, more or less, there is no need to look for any other meaning of 'order' than the chronological. The word *seder*, used here, has the meaning of chronological sequence elsewhere in the Rabbinic literature, as in the work on chronology entitled *Seder 'Olam* and in the statement 'there is no *seder* to the Mishnah,' i.e. the chapters of the Mishnah have not been arranged in any chronological sequence so that we cannot know which is earlier and which is later.[11]

If this is correct the whole thing hangs effectively together. First, there is the chronological order in which the Prophets lived; who came before whom. This is given as Joshua, Judges, Samuel, Kings, Jeremiah, Ezekiel, Isaiah and The Twelve. Then there is the chronological order of the *Ketuvim*, that is, the order in which the compilers of the various books lived. This is given as: Ruth, Psalms, Job, Proverbs, Ecclesiastes, Song of Songs, Lamentations, Daniel, Esther, Ezra and Chronicles, following the chronology of Samuel (author of Ruth), David (author of Psalms), David's son, Solomon (author of Proverbs, Ecclesiastes. Song of Songs), Jeremiah (author of Lamentations) and the Men of the Great Synagogue (the post-exilic authors of Daniel, Esther, Ezra and Chronicles). The third section on authorship cuts across the division between Prophets and *Ketuvim*, some of the Prophets being listed before some of the *Ketuvim*, unlike in the first two lists where all the Prophets are given and then all the *Ketuvim*, separately. Thus the chronological order in the authorship section is: Moses ('his' book, Balaam and Job); Joshua ('his' book and the last eight verses of the Torah); Samuel ('his' book Judges and Ruth); David (Psalms); Jeremiah ('his' book, Kings and Lamentations); Hezekiah and his associates (Isaiah and the three 'works of Solomon'); the Men of the Great Synagogue (Ezekiel, The Twelve, Daniel, Esther); and Ezra ('his' book and part of Chronicles; the rest completed by an unknown author).

The odd one out in the 'order' section is Isaiah. Chronologically, as the anonymous editors remark, Isaiah should come before Jeremiah and Ezekiel. The attempted solution to the difficulty, by the editors, is that the book of Jeremiah is a castigation of the people, foretelling their downfall. The first part of the book of Ezekiel has the same theme and hence is associated with Jeremiah. But Ezekiel concludes with a message of consolation and hence the book is appropriately followed by Isaiah which is consolation in its entirety. This 'solution' appears to be artificial. It is probably an echo of the way *Rabbinic* works were arranged.[12] Krochmal[13] has advanced the theory that in the original *baraita*, Isaiah is placed together with The Twelve because the early Rabbis recognised that in the book of Isaiah there is material belonging to the period of The Twelve and later even than Ezekiel. It seems improbable, however, that any of the ancient Rabbis entertained the notion of a Deutero-Isaiah. But if Krochmal's suggestion is modified somewhat, it does make sense, namely, that the Prophet Isaiah, *foresaw* events that were to occur after Ezekiel and in the time of some of The Twelve. Like their Christian near-contemporaries, the Rabbis believed that the Prophets could and did foretell the future in detail. Not for them was any suggestion that the Prophets were *forth*tellers rather than *fore*tellers. The only satisfactory way of accounting for Hezekiah coming after Jeremiah in the authorship section is that it is a parallel to the 'order' section where Isaiah, one of the books written by Hezekiah and his associates, comes after Jeremiah and Ezekiel. This would suggest that we have only one *baraita* or, at least, if we have three, they hang together.

That Job is placed first in the authorship section is, clearly, because the book is attributed to Moses. But why should it be third in the 'order' section, after Ruth and Psalms. The anonymous editors raise the question and give a similar answer to the one given in connection with Jeremiah and Ezekiel. This is that Job deals with human suffering and it is inappropriate to begin the list with a book having this theme. It is also possible that Job was placed in this order so as not to give too much prominence to a pagan hero.

On the question of authorship, the *baraita* states that Moses wrote 'his' book, that is, the Pentateuch. That Moses wrote the Pentateuch is, of course, taken for granted by the Rabbis. But, then, even the heretics, against whom the Rabbis fulminated for not believing that the Torah was from Heaven (*Torah min ha-Shamayyim*), had no doubts that Moses wrote the Pentateuch. The issue, in Rabbinic times, was not that of the Mosaic authorship of the Pentateuch. All, heretics and believers alike, accepted that it was Moses who actually wrote the Pentateuch. For the heretics he made it up out of his own head, for the believers God is the real author, Moses acting as His faithful scribe. This emerges from the discussion in tractate *Sanhedrin*[14] on the statement in the Mishnah that one who denies that the Torah is from Heaven has no share in the World to Come. Such an unbeliever, it is said, holds that Moses wrote some of it or all of it 'of his own accord,' *mi-pi 'atzmo*. Although in tractate *Megillah*[15] the statement occurs that Moses uttered the curses in Deuteronomy, unlike those in Leviticus, *me-'atzmo*, a similar expression to that used in the *Sanhedrin* passage, it surely cannot be taken to mean that Moses 'made up' the book of Deuteronomy, the belief castigated as rank heresy in *Sanhedrin*. And if that were the meaning, why only the curses in Deuteronomy and not the book as a whole? In all probability there is significance in the two different expressions used — *mi-pi 'atzmo* and *me-'atzmo*. The *Megillah* passage probably means no more that that in Deuteronomy Moses spoke as if he himself were conveying the message ('God will smite'), whereas in Leviticus God is made to take over more directly ('I will smite').

The *baraita* states that Joshua wrote the final eight verses dealing with the death of Moses. In our passage the editors quote another *baraita*[16] in which it is stated that this view — attributing the last eight verses to Joshua — is the opinion of 'either R. Judah or R. Nehemiah.' But R. Simeon holds that these verses, like the rest of the Torah, were written by Moses himself, with tears in his eyes at the contemplation of his own demise. To round off the picture, we must refer to the passage in tractate *Makkot* in which yet another *baraita* is quoted.[17] This reads: *And Joshua wrote these words in the book of the Law of God* (Joshua 24:26). R. Judah and R. Nehemiah are divided on the interpretation thereof; one holding that this refers to the last eight verses in the Torah (which Joshua added to the 'book of God's Torah'), while the other holds that it refers to the 'refuge cities.' The editors of *Makkot* express astonishment that any teacher can hold that a whole section of the Pentateuch, that dealing with the refuge cities, could have been written by anyone other than Moses himself. Consequently, they understand the reference to be the account of the refuge cities *in the book of Joshua* (Joshua 20:1–9), which Joshua wrote in *his* book, even though the original law is in the Torah written by

Moses. In all probability, by the time the Talmud was edited, it had become inconceivable that Joshua or anyone else could have added to the Torah, except, according to one opinion, the account of Moses' death. But it seems highly probable, taking the two *baraitot* together, that the meaning is rather that R. Judah and R. Nehemiah both disagree with R. Simeon, holding that a section of the Torah was written by Joshua; one of the two holding that the section added by Joshua is the account of Moses' death, the other that it is the passage about the refuge cities (Numbers 35:9–34; Deuteronomy 19:1–13) which, on this view, could not have been written by Moses since all the refuge cities did not come into Israel's possession until the conquest by Joshua.

If this analysis is correct, it follows that in the second half of the second century CE (the period of R. Judah, R. Nehemiah and R. Simeon) it was still possible to maintain that there are post-Mosaic additions to the Pentateuch. But by approximately the fifth century in Babylon, the probable date when the final framework to the Talmud was provided by the anonymous editors, it had become axiomatic that only the final eight verses could have been written by Joshua, so that the reference to the refuge cities had to be reinterpreted as applying not to the passage in the Pentateuch, but to the passage in the book of Joshua.

It is also worth noting that even the editors of the Talmud do not appeal to dogmatic considerations. They do not protest that it offends against basic Jewish beliefs to maintain that the account of the refuge cities in the Pentateuch had been added after Moses. All they do is to affirm that this is untenable on 'historical' grounds, i.e. no one holds that view. To repeat what has already been said, the dogmatic aspect has to do with inspiration, whether the Torah is 'from Heaven' or 'made up' by Moses. Of course, the Rabbis did believe that Moses wrote the Pentateuch but, then, in their day everyone believed this, even the 'heretic.' A good illustration of how this kind of distinction was made in Rabbinic times is provided by the discussion[18] whether the book of Ecclesiastes 'contaminates the hands,' i.e. whether it is sacred Scripture. Those who hold that it is sacred Scripture believe that it was compiled by Solomon under the influence of the 'holy spirit' (*ruaḥ ha-kodesh*). Those who hold that it is no part of sacred Scripture to do so because, in their opinion, it is the uninspired 'wisdom of Solomon.' For both it is accepted implicitly that King Solomon is the author of the book.

In other words, contrary to many modern views on the subject, the ancient Rabbis in no way sought to engage in Biblical criticism. As we have noted, questions of authorship of the Biblical books were only of peripheral interest to them. They did not admit the question into their consideration of dogma and certainly did not purport to be conveying a tradition. Thus to see in the passage we are examining, a Jewish tradition but a very faulty one is to miss the point entirely.[19] It was never intended as conveying an authentic tradition any more than legends in the Rabbinic Midrash are intended to report actual happenings in the lives, say, of the Patriarchs, Moses and David.

Very curious is the statement in our *baraita* that Moses wrote the portion of Balaam. In the only other parallel to this statement, the Jerusalem Talmud[20] puts it rather more clearly: 'Moses wrote five books of the Torah and then he wrote the portion about Balak and Balaam and then he wrote the book of Job.' The Jerusalem Talmud evidently understands the statement to mean that first Moses wrote 'his' book, i.e. the rest of the Pentateuch, after which he wrote the other two books, those of Balaam and Job. In both the Jerusalem Talmud and in our *baraita* the portion of Balaam, although written by Moses, is treated as a separate 'book' (probably because it is the account of a prophet other than Moses), but in both all 'six' books are part of the divinely dictated Torah, unlike the book of Job, which, even though written by Moses, is only inspired by God in the lesser degree of inspiration known as 'the holy spirit' (*ruah ha-kodesh*) typical of the other books of the *Ketuvim*, which is why in our *baraita* it belongs among the *Ketuvim*.

On the manner in which the Pentateuch was written by Moses, there is a debate[21] between the third-century Palestinian teachers, R. Johanan and Resh Lakish; one holding that each part of the Torah was 'given,' i.e. dictated by God for Moses to record in writing, at the time when the events related in it took place (*Torah megillah megillah nitenah*); the other holding that it was all dictated and written down at one time towards the end of the forty-years journey through the wilderness (*Torah hatumah nitenah*). Contrary to the opinion widely held by Orthodox Jews today and repeated by some modern scholars, the Rabbinic doctrine, 'The Torah is from Sinai',[22] does not mean that, in the Rabbinic view, the whole of the Pentateuch was 'given' at Sinai, only that the laws and doctrines contained in the Written and Oral Torah (*Torah she-be-'al peh*) were given at Sinai. Nowhere in the whole of the Rabbinic literature is it stated, grossly anachronistically (how could it be?), that God dictated to Moses at Sinai accounts of events yet to take place.

The statement in our *baraita* that Samuel wrote Judges and Ruth as well as his own book is not presented as a tradition but is clearly based on the idea that Samuel recorded the history of his people to his own day, and since the books of Judges and Ruth are part of that history it is assumed that Samuel wrote them down.

The ten elders said in the *baraita* to have contributed to the book of Psalms are either the persons mentioned in the superscriptions to certain Psalms or 'found' to be authors by the *midrashic* process. Thus Adam is found in Psalm 139:16, *Thine eyes did see mine imperfect substance*, referring to the clay from which Adam was moulded. Melchizedek appears in Psalm 110:4, *'al divrati malk-hizedek*, understood as *by my word, I Melchizedek*. To Moses is attributed Psalm 90 because of the superscription: *A Prayer of Moses the man of God*. As for Abraham, the anonymous editors point to the *midrashic* identification of Ethan the Ezrahite, in the superscription of Psalm 89, with the patriarch Abraham. Hemen appears in the superscription to Psalm 88; Yeduthun in the superscription to Psalms 39, 62 and 77; Asaph in the superscription to Psalms 50 and 73–83. The three sons of Korah occur in the superscription to Psalms 42, 44, 49, 85, 87 and 88. The ten elders, then, are: Adam, Melchizedek, Moses, Abraham, Heman, Yeduthun, Asaph and the three sons of Korah. That there were three sons of Korah is based on the naming of the three sons of the Korah who rebelled against Moses; their names are given as Assir, Elkanah and Abiasaph (Exodus 6:24).[23] The artificiality of all this is startling until we realise that it was intended in order to find somehow ten elders, ten being, of course, the sacred number. This is stated explicitly in the *midrash* to Psalms,[24] 'Just as the Psalms bear the names of ten authors, so do they bear also the name of ten kinds of song.'

Although there is an acknowledgement of the composite nature of the book of Psalms, this is hardly due to a critical examination by the Rabbis. The superscriptions state this, in any event, and all the *baraita* does is to bring up the number to ten. All ten elders lived before David who incorporated the work they had composed into his book of Psalms. It is necessary to repeat that the Rabbis were not Bible critics before their time. There is no suggestion here or anywhere else in the Rabbinic literature that there are post-Davidic additions to the book of Psalms. Psalm 137, for instance, is interpreted in the Midrash as King David's prophetic vision.[25] There is, however, a single statement in the *midrash*, dealing with the ten elders who composed Psalms, which seems to tell against this contention. In the passage,[26] instead of Melchizedek, Ezra is given as one of the ten. But this is so contrary to the usual Rabbinic view and, indeed, to the whole thrust of the Midrash that David 'used' the work of predecessors, that it is almost certain that an error has crept into the *midrashic* text. It is, I think, a plausible conjecture that 'Ezra' is a textual error for Ethan the *Ezra*hite, identified in our passage with Abraham but not mentioned at all in our texts of the Midrash.[27]

The reference to Jeremiah writing the books of Kings and Lamentations is similarly based on the idea that the Prophet brought the history down to his own day, but not necessarily in a single book.

Generally in the Rabbinic literature, Proverbs, Ecclesiastes and Song of Songs are presumed to be 'the words' of Solomon,[28] i.e. he is responsible for the inspired words, but these were not written down by him but by Hezekiah and his associates. This is obviously based on the title of Proverbs 25: *These are the proverbs, which the men of Hezekiah king of Judah copied down.* A distinction is made in the whole *baraita* and in Rabbinic literature generally between the authorship of a book and its recording in writing. God 'spoke' the Torah and Moses wrote it down; the ten elders uttered their Psalms and David wrote them down as part of his book: Solomon 'spoke' his parables and the other two books are also his 'words,' but the actual writing was done by Hezekiah and his associates.

That the Men of the Great Synagogue wrote the books of Ezekiel, The Twelve, Daniel and Esther is because the majority of the material in these books is post-Exilic and the Men of the Great Synagogue functioned after the return.

The great French commentator to *Bava Batra*, Rashi, first remarks that he does not know why it is said that Ezekiel did not write his own book. He goes on to hazard a guess that since Ezekiel prophesied outside the Holy Land, he could not write down his prophesies to become sacred literature. This had to be done by the Men of the Great Synagogue in the Holy Land.

In our *baraita* Daniel belongs to the *Ketuvim*; unlike in the Septuagint where the book of Daniel is found at the end of the Prophets. This is because, in the Rabbinic view generally, Daniel was not a prophet,[29] but was possessed of the lesser degree of inspiration known as the 'holy spirit' (*ruah ha-kodesh*), typical of the *Ketuvim*.

Perhaps this chapter is best concluded with a brief note on how the *baraita* fared in medieval Jewish exegesis. By this time, statements in the Talmud regarding the authorship of the Biblical books had come to be accepted in wide circles as revealed truth. This was the result of the increasing reverence for the Talmud as the holy work second only to the Bible, and for the Talmudic Rabbis who tended to be seen as infallible, spiritual supermen. It became virtually a dogma that the Biblical books were written by the men to whom they are attributed in the 'tradition,' that is, chiefly by our *baraita*.

Yet even in the Middle Ages teachers were to be found who treated the *baraita* as they treated other Talmudic views on what happened in the past; as history to be examined and rejected if necessary by the light of reason, not to be accepted as belonging to the dogmas of the Jewish religion. Thus Abraham Ibn Ezra[30] purported to detect certain post-Mosaic additions to the Pentateuch other than the last eight verses. Judah the Saint of Regensburgh could say, without the slightest suggestion that he was a daring iconoclast, that Genesis 36:39 and 48:20 may have been glosses added by the Men of the Great Synagogue, and that Psalm 136 was originally in the Pentateuch at Numbers 21:17, from whence David took it, as he took Psalm 90, and incorporated it in the book of Psalms.[31] Abarbanel[32] can write, in contradiction to our *baraita*, it is extremely unlikely that Joshua wrote the book of Joshua. These exegetes, unlike the compilers of the *baraita*, were engaged in a rudimentary form of Biblical criticism and Ibn Ezra, in particular, has good claim to be considered its real pioneer, as Spinoza acknowledged. It is only necessary to compare their approach with that of the Talmudic Rabbis to see the very different nature of the Talmudic activity. When, in our *baraita* and elsewhere, the Talmudic and *midrashic* Rabbis refer to this or that person writing this or that book of the Bible, their interest was of no greater significance for them than when they discussed other events of the distant past. All their work, therefore, in this area has little relevance for the study of the Bible itself. We have tried to show, however, that it has a good deal of relevance to the study of the study of Bible.

4

Literary analysis of the *sugya* in *Bava Kama* 11a–12b

This chapter seeks to apply literary analysis to a Talmudic *sugya* with a view to noting how the editors of the Babylonian Talmud shaped their material in order to provide a structured unit. The *sugya* is in tractate *Bava Kama* 11a–12b, paralleled, in its first section, by the *sugya* in the *Yerushalmi*, *Kiddushin* 1:4 (60b–c).

The *sugya* begins with a discussion regarding a *ganav* ('sneak thief') or a *gazlan* ('robber') who has stolen an animal which then dies while in his possession. Obviously he must compensate the owner, but the question discussed is what is the form this compensation takes. Does the thief have to refund the value the animal had while alive or can he return the carcass and pay only the difference between the value of the live animal and the carcass? If the latter, the court makes an assessment of the difference in value, hence this method of payment is called 'they make an assessment' (*shamin*). Now on the basis of an inference from the *mishnah* (*Bava Kama* 1:2) the rule is that, in the case where a man kills or injures his neighbour's animal, the more lenient method of payment, that is *shamin*, is said to be the rule. Consequently, the *sugya* is appended to this *mishnah*. After the statement (*Bava Kama* 10b–11a) that *shamin* is the rule in the case of damages, the *sugya* proceeds to discuss whether there is *shamin* in the case of the *ganav* and *gazlan* or whether here, unlike in the case of damages, full payment has to be made (*eyn shamin*).

After a statement on the question by Samuel and a discussion on this, the Talmud continues with the ruling of Ulla in the name of R. Eleazar[1] that no assessment is made in the case of the *ganav* and the *gazlan* (*eyn shamin*). In the far from unusual style of the Talmud, a number of further rulings given by Ulla in the name of R. Eleazar are quoted and each discussed in turn. These rulings have no apparent connection with one another. The topics are diverse, the sole connecting thread being, evidently, the attribution to Ulla in the name of R. Eleazar.

The first ruling of Ulla in the name of R. Eleazar is, as stated, on the question of *shamin*. The second ruling concerns a placenta (*shilya*) that emerged partly on one day and partly on the next day. The question here is whether it can be assumed that the major part of the foetus emerged in the placenta on the first day. If it can be so assumed, it would be counted as if the woman had given birth from the first day so that her days of impurity after childbirth (Leviticus 12:1–8) are counted from that day. Ulla in the name of R. Eleazar rules that the count is from the first day, and a brief discussion follows on the question of whether it can really be assumed that the placenta contained the major part of the foetus.

The third ruling quoted of Ulla in the name of R. Eleazar concerns a first-born who dies within thirty days of his birth, that is before the date of which, if he had lived, he would have required to have been redeemed (Numbers 18:15).[2] Ulla in the name of R. Eleazar rules that no redemption is required and the Talmud supports this ruling from a *baraita*.

The fourth ruling of Ulla in the name of R. Eleazar concerns the mode by which a large animal, a horse, ox or camel, is acquired. Ulla states in the name of R. Eleazar that the mode of acquisition (the *kinyan*) is that of leading the animal (*meshikhah*), that is, the transfer is not effected until the purchaser has led the animal from the possession of the seller. The Talmud raises an objection from the *mishnah* (*Kiddushin* 1:4) in which it is stated that the mode of acquisition for a large animal is 'handing over' (*mesirah*), that is, the mere handing over of the reins suffices to effect the transfer and *meshikhah* has no validity whatsoever. To this the reply is given that, contrary to the *mishnah*, there is a *baraita* in which the Sages rule that *meshikhah* is the operative mode of acquisition and R. Eleazar follows the *baraita*.

The fifth ruling of Ulla in the name of R. Eleazar concerns brothers who are heirs to their father's estate and wish to divide up the estate among them. For this an assessment has to be made by the court. Such assessment is called, as in the first instance of Ulla in the name of R. Eleazar, *shamin*. Ulla's ruling in the name of R. Eleazar is that while the clothes the brothers wear have to be assessed, the clothes worn by their sons and daughters remain theirs without them having to suffer the indignity of having evaluated the very garments on their backs. The Talmud adds that R. Pappa observed, if there is an older brother who has been conducting the affairs of the estate

43

on behalf of all of them, he can retain the clothes he wears without them having to be assessed, since, it can be assumed, the other brothers had waived their rights, content to let him wear more impressive clothes in order for him to appear in dignified habit when conducting the business of the estate.

The sixth ruling of Ulla in the name of R. Eleazar concerns a bailee who appoints another bailee to act in his stead without consulting the bailor. For example, A appoints B to be a bailee for A's animal and B hands the animal over to C to act as a bailee. The animal then suffers an accident. Now if B had not given the animal to another bailee, he would not be held responsible in law for any damage suffered as a result of the accident since he had not been negligent. But here, it can be argued, the very act of handing the animal over to an unauthorised person constitutes negligence in itself and the bailee is liable. Ulla states in R. Eleazar's name that the bailee is not liable. The Talmud elaborates, even if the first bailee had been hired for the purpose, and is a *shomer sakhar*, that is, one whose degree of responsibility is greater, and the second bailee is a gratuitous bailee (*shomer ḥinam*), that is, with a lesser degree of responsibility, the first bailee is still not liable since, after all, he had handed the animal over to an intelligent person and cannot be said to have broken his contract. But, the Talmud continues, Rava holds that the first bailee is liable. On this too the Talmud elaborates. Even if the first bailee is a gratuitous bailee and the second a hired bailee, the first is liable. This is because if a bailee declares that an accident has occurred to the animal he had agreed to look after, he must take an oath to that effect. Consequently, the owner of the animal, in our case, can refuse to accept the word of the second bailee, even on oath, that an accident had occurred and that it was not due to negligence. He trusted the first bailee by asking him to be a bailee, but having had no contractual arrangement with the second bailee, why should he take his word? To be noted here is the carefully constructed pattern. The elaboration on Ulla in the name of R. Eleazar is arranged so as to be symmetrically opposed by the elaboration on Rava's ruling.

Finally, there is a ruling of Ulla in the name of R. Eleazar on the much-discussed question of whether there is a lien on slaves. If A lends B money and B cannot repay, A can claim the amount owing to him from property B had sold to C subsequent to his having incurred the debt. Similarly, if B had died, A can claim from B's estate.

But this only applies to real estate (*karka'*) not to moveables (*metaltelin*). There is a lien on *karka'* (lit. 'land') but not on *metaltelin* ('moveables'). What is the position with regard to slaves? Are slaves treated, in law, as *karka*,' on which there is lien, or as *metaltelin*, on which there is no lien? Ulla is quoted as saying in the name of R. Eleazar, 'The law is (*hilketha*) that a debt can be recovered from slaves,' evidently because slaves are treated as real estate.

It is somewhat odd that only this statement, of the seven by Ulla in the name of R. Eleazar, is prefaced with the word *hilketha*, 'The law is.' This word is, in all probability, not R. Eleazar's but has been added by the editors. It is in Aramaic, unlike the rest of the statement, and the other six statements, which are in Hebrew. This is no doubt because, as the *sugya* proceeds to demonstrate, there is considerable debate on this question, so that the editors are really saying: despite the debate on the issue, R. Eleazar *rules* that slaves are treated as real estate. It is worth noting that in tractate *Bava Batra* (128a–129a), there is a series of rulings sent by R. Abba to R. Joseph b. Hama, the first of which is that a debt can be collected from slaves. In this and the next ruling the word *halakhah* (in Hebrew) precedes the ruling. This is no doubt for the same reason we have suggested, because the matter is strongly debated. Moreover, in *Bava Batra* the Talmud continues that R. Nahman disagrees and this fits in with our *sugya* where R. Nahman takes issue with Ulla. (It is possible that there is, in fact, in the *Bava Batra* passage, a cross reference to our *sugya*. It may even be that *hilketha* in our *sugya* is not the original, but has been added later from *Bava Batra*. It is perhaps not entirely coincidental that this word occurs in the *sugya* immediately preceding this one and again later in the *sugya*.)

The pattern of the whole *sugya* is as follows:

1 First saying of Ulla: *shamin*, connected with *shamin* in the case of damages.
2 Second saying of Ulla: *shilya*, discussed.
3 Third saying of Ulla: the first-born, supported by a *baraita*.
4 Fourth saying of Ulla: large animal with *meshikhah*, but contradicted by the *mishnah*? Reply: R. Eleazar follows the *baraita*.
5 Fifth saying of Ulla: assessment (*shamin*) of the clothes; qualification by R. Pappa.
6 Sixth saying of Ulla: the bailee is not liable. Elaboration of this, even if first bailee a *shomer sakhar* and the second a *shomer ḥinam*. Rava's ruling: the first bailee is liable. Elaboration of this, even

if first bailee is a *shomer ḥinam* and the second a *shomer sakhar*.

7 Seventh saying of Ulla: a debt can be collected from slaves.

Apart from the actual sayings of R. Eleazar and the Tannaitic sources quoted in the course of the discussion, the whole of the *sugya* is the work of the final editors. It is futile to consider whether there is any connection between the seven items apart from the attribution to Ulla in the name of R. Eleazar. The linking of diverse topics solely because they have a common authorship is a frequent literary device in the Babylonian Talmud,[3] and the attempts by commentators to find a linking theme in such instances is misguided.[4]

A question now to be considered is, are there any other sayings of Ulla in the name of R. Eleazar in the Babylonian Talmud and, if there are, why are these not included in the list given in our *sugya*? After consulting the Concordance,[5] we find the following six further instances of Ulla quoting R. Eleazar in the Babylonian Talmud:

1 *'Eruvin* 21b and *Yevamot* 21a

Ulla said in the name of R. Eleazar:[6] 'The Torah was at first like a basket which had no handles until Solomon came and fixed handles to it.'

2 *Pesaḥim* 70b

Ulla said in the name of R. Eleazar: 'If peace-offerings were killed on the eve of the Festival, they can count neither as *simḥah* offerings nor as *ḥagigah* offerings.'

3 *Gittin* 20a

Ulla said in the name of R. Eleazar: 'Graving is invalid if the letters are in relief but valid if they are hollowed out.'

4 *Sanhedrin* 16a

Ulla said in the name of R. Eleazar: 'This refers to a dispute over the division of land.'

5 Zevaḥim 14b

Ulla said in the name of R. Eleazar: 'It is invalid if the blood of a sacrifice is taken to the altar by a non-priest.'

6 Hullin 137b

Ulla said in the name of R. Eleazar: 'Our *mishnah* states "whatever".' (A reference to the statement in the *mishnah*, Ḥullin 11:2, that whatever the weight of the first shearings of the sheep, the priest must receive his portion. Other Amoraim do not take 'whatever' literally and hold there are limits to the obligation.)

Assuming that the editors of our *sugya* knew of these six further sayings in the name of R. Eleazar, why did they omit them from the list? Number 1 is *aggadic* and hardly fits into a list of *halakhic* rulings. Numbers 3, 4 and 6 are not statements but attempts at explicating the meaning of a Tannaitic source. Numbers 2 and 5 are *halakhic* rulings, but have to do with the sacrificial system and are inappropriate in a list of practical rulings such as the list in our *sugya*. But, as we shall see from the *sugya* in the *Yerushalmi*, the list in our *sugya* is not the work of the editors so that the question, in any event, is not why the editors omitted the other six items; though the reason we have suggested may well be why the other six did not feature in R. Eleazar's original list. Again, as we shall see, the original list of R. Eleazar was drawn up as replies to a series of questions sent to him by R. Judah from Babylon, forming a separate unit, independent of any other sayings Ulla attributed to R. Eleazar.

To turn now to the *Yerushalmi*: this *sugya* has the identical list (with one addition to be noted presently), but this is appended to the *mishnah* in *Kiddushin* on the acquisition of a large animal. Consequently, this item features first in the list in the *Yerushalmi*, whereas in our *sugya* the case of *shamin* features first in the list since it is appended to the *mishnah* in *Bava Kama* out of which the question of *shamin* arose.

With regard to all the items in the *Yerushalmi* list, except the first, the opening formula of each item is, 'R. Judah sent to ask R. Eleazar,' and then R. Eleazar's reply is given. With regard to the first item, the *Yerushalmi* simply states, 'R. Judah sent,' without any reference to whom he sent the query. It can be conjectured that the omission

47

of R. Eleazar in this instance is simply due to the copyist, but even if R. Eleazar's name was not in the original text it is clear from the whole context that the meaning is here, too, that R. Eleazar is the teacher to whom R. Judah sent his query. Thus we have a number of questions that R. Judah in Babylon sent to R. Eleazar in Palestine for the latter's opinion. The fact that R. Eleazar's replies are given in the form *amar leh*, 'he said to him,' does not mean, of course, that he *said* it to him directly, only that he communicated it to him by a third party who visited Babylon. In all probability, the visitor was none other than Ulla who was one of the *naḥotey*, the Palestinian teachers who came to Babylon and communicated to the Babylonians the teachings of the great Palestinian Amoraim.[7] This explains adequately why, in our *sugya*, the list of R. Eleazar's sayings is attributed to Ulla.

It should also be noted that in the *Yerushalmi* version, R. Eleazar rules that a large animal is acquired by *mesirah* (as in the *mishnah*) and not by *meshikhah* as in our *sugya*.[8] In the case of the bailee, the *Yerushalmi* version has it that R. Eleazar holds that the first bailee is liable, whereas in our *sugya* R. Eleazar rules that he is not liable. In our *sugya*, in the case of the *ganav* and *gazlan*, R. Eleazar rules that no assessment is made (*eyn shamin*), whereas in the *Yerushalmi* version R. Eleazar rules that an assessment is made (though the *Yerushalmi* does not use the term *shamin*). Evidently, although both the *Bavli* and the *Yerushalmi* know of the same items, they diverge as to what R. Eleazar actually said with regard to three of them. In other words, the items are the same in both Talmuds, but the actual wording of R. Eleazar's statements is that of the respective editors.

In the *Yerushalmi* version there is an additional item. This also concerns brothers who divide their father's estate among themselves. Both the father and one of the brothers dies, the latter without issue. The remaining brothers divide up among themselves both the father's estate and that of the deceased brother to whom they are the heirs, since he died without issue. One of the surviving brothers then performs levirate marriage. The question is whether the levir, now in the place of the deceased brother whose widow he has married, can reclaim from the other brothers all that they have taken from that brother's estate. R. Eleazar rules that they do not have to relinquish their share in the deceased brother's estate.

The following is the list as it appears in the *Yerushalmi*. As in the

Bavli, there is editorial discussion on each of the items:

1 The case of the large animal, acquired by *mesirah.*
2 The case of the first-born infant.
3 The case of the *shilya.*
4 The case of the bailee.
5 The brothers who divide the estate: the case of the levir.
6 The brothers who divide the estate: the case of the clothing.[9]
7 The case of claiming the debt from slaves.
8 Assessment in the case of *ganav* or *gazlan.*

The omission of Number 5 from our *sugya* requires an explanation. It is surely unlikely that the editors of the *Bavli* knew all the other items in the list except for this one. It is possible that the editors of the *Bavli* version did, in fact, know that there were two items about brothers dividing up their father's estate, but saw fit to record and discuss only one so as to make the list one of seven items and no more. There are other examples in the *Bavli* of a fondness for structuring a *sugya* around certain 'sacred' or formal numbers, three, five and seven, for example.[10]

The order in which the various items in the *Yerushalmi* list are presented would seem to be arbitrary, except for the first item. This must come first since, in the *Yerushalmi,* the list is appended to the *mishnah* in *Kiddushin* which deals with this item, the mode of acquisition of a large animal. Is the order in our *sugya* in the *Bavli* similarly arbitrary or is it possible to see the sequence as intentional and contrived.[11]

It would seem that the first and last items, at least, are placed in their position intentionally; the first because it is the link with the *mishnah* to which the whole list is appended, and the last because it leads on to the lengthy discussion on whether slaves are to be treated as real estate or as moveables (11b–12b). This latter is really a separate *sugya,* deserving separate treatment, which could not have been given to it had it been inserted, as in the *Yerushalmi,* somewhere within the list. Can any particular sequence be discovered in the arrangement of the other five items? Highly conjectural though it is, there is the possibility that items 2 and 3 are placed in this order (unlike the *Yerushalmi* where the order of these two items is reversed) because the *shilya* case concerns an infant about to be born, while the case of the first-born is of an infant who dies after a proper birth. But it is difficult to discover any reason for the order in which the next three items are arranged.

The second part of the *sugya* opens with R. Nahman asking Ulla: 'When R. Eleazar stated that there can be distraint on slaves did he mean to imply that even where the debtor had died, the debt can be collected from the heirs?' That is to say, does R. Eleazar hold that slaves are treated as real estate? To this Ulla replies: 'No. Only from the debtor himself.' To this reply the objection is raised: 'If from the debtor himself, why mention slaves in particular since all the debtor's property is in pledge?' To this the reply is given that the case is where the debtor had agreed for a mortgage to be placed on the slaves. Here the slaves, even if treated as moveables, can be claimed from the purchaser (and hence from the heirs as well). In support, the opinion of Rava is quoted. Rava rules that where there is a mortgage on slaves the slaves can be claimed from the purchaser, but where there is a mortgage on an ox it cannot be claimed from the purchaser. The reason for the distinction is given. Where there is a mortgage on slaves people know about it, but where there is a mortgage on an ox people do not normally know about it, and it would be unfair to the purchaser if the ox can be collected from him.[12] Presumably, the meaning here is that this is called 'from him' since it is the debtor who agreed for the mortgage on the slaves.[13] The Talmud continues that when R. Nahman had left, Ulla declared that R. Eleazar did say that slaves can be claimed even from the heirs (even where they were not mortgaged), since slaves are treated as real estate. When R. Nahman heard of this, he declared that Ulla had avoided his displeasure by giving an evasive reply to his question.

There now follows a statement on the practical consequences of R. Nahman's debate with Ulla. The case of the slaves came up in Nehardea and the judges of Nehardea ruled that slaves can be distrained. There was another case in Pumbedita and R. Hana b. Bizna gave the same ruling. But R. Nahman ordered these judges to reverse their decisions, otherwise he would take their own houses from them to recompense the purchasers. Rava then asked R. Nahman on what authority did he decide against Ulla, R. Eleazar and the other judges, to which R. Nahman replied that he relies on a *baraita* quoted by Avimi. This *baraita* states that a *prosbol* (the declaration to the court which allows a lender to claim his debt after the Year of Release) can be drawn up if the lender has land (*karka'*), but not if he has only slaves. A second statement in the *baraita* is with regard to the law that when A sells B land and moveables, no separate act of acquisition is required for the moveables. The transfer of the moveable property is effected automatically by virtue of the act of acquisition which transfers the land. But, states the *baraita*, if A sold B slaves and moveables, the acquisition of the slaves is ineffective for the transfer of the moveables. Both these rulings of the *baraita* support R. Nahman's view that slaves are treated as moveables not as land.

Having established that there is a debate between R. Nahman and the others on whether slaves are treated as real estate or as moveables, and having R. Nahman's quote from Avimi's *baraita*, the Talmud now proceeds to discuss whether, in fact, a debate on the question had already taken place in Tannaitic circles. Two further *baraitot* are quoted. The first *baraita* gives the following rules regarding simultaneous acquisition of property. If A sold B land and slaves, a separate act of acquisition has to be made for each. The act of acquisition of the land is ineffective for the slaves and *vice versa*. If he sold land and moveables the act of acquisition of the land suffices for the moveables, but the acquisition of the moveables is ineffective for the land. If he sold slaves and moveables, the act of acquisition for either is ineffective for the other. Thus we have a *baraita* in which, evidently, slaves are treated as moveables, since if they are treated as land the act of acquisition of the slaves should be effective for the moveables. This *baraita* is in accord with Avimi's *baraita* and with R. Nahman's opinion. But in another *baraita* the opposite opinion is stated, that the act of acquisition of the slaves is effective for the transfer of the moveables. Evidently, the first *baraita*, in which it is stated that the act of acquisition of the slaves is ineffective for the moveables, holds that slaves are treated as moveables, while the second *baraita*, in which it is stated that it is effective, holds that slaves are treated as real estate. Thus the question seems to have been debated among the Tannaim.

R. Ika son of R. Ammi retorts that it does not necessarily follow that the two *baraitot* are debating the question whether slaves are treated as land or as moveables. It may well be that both *baraita* hold that slaves are treated as land for other purposes, such as in the case of Ulla and R. Eleazar. In that case why does the first *baraita* rule that the act of acquisition of the slaves is ineffective for the moveables? R. Ika argues that *kinyan agav* (the acquisition of moveables through the acquisition of land) is in a different category, according to this *baraita*. The principle of *kinyan agav* is stated in the *mishnah* (*Kiddushin* 1:5). The Amora Hezekiah states that the rule is derived[14] from the verse: *And their father gave them great gifts of silver and gold and of precious things with fortified cities in Judah* (2 Chronicles 21:3). Hezekiah understands the word 'with' in the verse as stating the rule of *kinyan agav*, i.e. the moveables were acquired 'together with' the fortified cities, and no separate act of acquisition was required for the transfer of the moveables to be effective. Since the paradigm is 'fortified cities,' the *baraita* holds, then even if in other cases slaves are treated as land, they cannot be so treated in this case. They may be legal 'land' but here real land, like the fortified cities, is required; in the language of the Talmud, 'land that does not move.'

There now follows a different version of what R. Ika said in order to deal with the contradiction between the two *baraitot*. In this version both *baraitot* hold that slaves are treated as moveables. The first *baraita*, in which it is stated that the act of acquisition of the slaves is ineffective for the moveables is now perfectly intelligible. But why does the second *baraita* state that it is effective? The answer is, according to this version of R. Ika, because this *baraita* does not deal with *kinyan agav* at all, but with the case where the moveables are actually worn by the slaves or are otherwise on the slaves' person. The reason why the act of acquisition of the slaves is effective for the moveables is because the slave becomes the 'courtyard' (*hatzer*) of the purchaser and whatever is in a man's courtyard is acquired automatically by him. It is as if A sold B a courtyard and all its contents. No separate act of acquisition is required for the contents.

At this stage of the discussion, it has been suggested that a slave can serve as a 'courtyard,' a *hatzer*, for the purpose of acquisition. But, the Talmud now objects, to qualify as a 'courtyard' for this purpose the object must not move, otherwise it is a 'moveable *hatzer*' (*hatzer mehalekhet* 'a walking courtyard') and a moveable courtyard is ineffective for the purpose. If you will reply, continues the Talmud, that the case is where the slave is stationary (and hence he is not a 'moving courtyard') this will not do, since Rava[15] has ruled that a *hatzer* which cannot acquire while it is moving cannot acquire even when it is stationary (i.e. it is still a *moveable* courtyard). To this the Talmud replies, *ve-hilketha be-kafut*, 'And the law is where the slave is bound' i.e. and cannot move.[16]

The Talmud now turns to the clause in the first *baraita* to the effect that the act of acquisition of the land is ineffective for the slaves. But a third *baraita* is now quoted in which it is stated that it is effective. To this the reply is given that this *baraita* deals with the case of slaves actually on the land at the time of acquisition. Where the slaves are actually on the land, no separate act of acquisition is required for them. But where they are not on the land, the act of acquisition for the land is ineffective for the slaves.

It has been suggested at this stage of the discussion that the first *baraita* states that while the acquisition of land is effective for moveables (because of *kinyan agav*), it is ineffective for the acquisition of slaves. And we have the two versions of R. Ika. In one of these, this *baraita* holds that slaves are treated as real estate. In the other, they are treated as moveables. Now if the second version of R. Ika is accepted as the authentic one, the *baraita* holds that slaves are treated as moveables. Hence, it can be argued, the act of acquisition of the land is ineffective for the slaves, because the rule of *kinyan agav* might only apply where the moveables are on the land. But according to the first version of R. Ika, the *baraita* holds that slaves are as real estate, and hence the sale of land and slaves is akin to the sale of two parcels of land in different spots. But in this case Samuel has stated that if ten fields are sold together, even if they are in ten different districts, the act of acquisition of any one is effective for all the others. In that case, why does the *baraita* rule that the slaves are not acquired through the land?

The Talmud retorts, but there is a difficulty even according to R. Ika's second version. It cannot be maintained that *kinyan agav* is only effective where the moveables are actually on the land. This is not so since 'we have established the rule'[17] that 'we do not require *tzibburin*' (that the moveables be 'heaped up' on the land for *kinyan agav* to be operative). Perforce, it must be said that slaves are in a category of their own. Although other moveables are not required to be actually on the land for *kinyan agav* to operate, slaves are required to be on the land. The distinction is between moveables that are inert, and moveables such as slaves (in this version treated not as land but as moveables) which 'wander' (*nayedey*, the same word used earlier in the *sugya* in connection with the distinction between the fortified cities and the slaves). The rule of *kinyan agav* cannot apply to slaves unless they are actually on the land, not when they are away from the land and can 'wander' away of their own accord. By the same token, there is no difficulty if the second version of R. Ika is accepted. Although, in this version, the *baraita* holds that slaves are like land, and although Samuel has said that to acquire land in one place is effective for land in another place, yet slaves are in a different category because they 'wander' (*nayedey*). The ten fields in Samuel's case are all interconnected, since they are, after all, on the same earth as all other land. But the slaves are in no way connected with the land together with which they are sold, and hence the act of acquisition of the land is ineffective for the slaves.

The pattern of this second part of our *sugya* is then as follows:

1 R. Nahman relies on Avimi's *baraita*: slaves are like moveables.
2 Is this debated by Tannaim? Two *baraitot* quoted: *baraita* A: land and slaves ineffective. *baraita* B: slaves and moveables effective because A holds slaves like moveables and B holds slaves like land.
3 R. Ika, first version: both A and B hold slaves like land; B no problem. As for A: slaves not like 'fortified cities.'
4 R. Ika, second version: both A and B hold slaves like moveables; A no problem. As for B: moveables are on the slaves. But a slave is a moving *hatzer*? And even if stationary, as Rava says. The slave is bound.
5 *Baraita* quoted: land and slaves effective but in A ineffective? The slaves are on the land.
6 But this correct only according to R. Ika, second version according to R. Ika, first version should be like ten fields (Samuel).
7 But even according to R. Ika, second version, no need for slaves to be on the land?
8 Hence distinction must be made between land and slaves and here, too, same distinction.

It can be seen at a glance that the *sugya* has been intentionally structured to a pattern. Each *baraita*[18] and each version of R. Ika is introduced at exactly the right moment to provide a neat, symmetrical arrangement; just as in a symphony each instrument is introduced when the harmony requires it. Also to be noted is the way in which there is a subtle play on that which is 'on it' and that which is away; between that which 'wanders' and that which does not. There is a strong element of artificiality about the whole structure but that is precisely the point. It is this which produces the dramatic effect. The whole is presented, to vary the metaphor, rather like a poem; not a poem of words but of ideas.

5

Literary analysis of the *sugya* in *Bava Kama* 20a–21a

The *sugya* examined here (*Bava Kama* 20a–21a) is appended to the *mishnah* (*Bava Kama* 2:2), wherein the ruling is given that the owner of an animal which eats food lying in the public domain is not obliged to compensate the owner of the food for his loss. This is because the type of damage done by the animal through eating is known as *shen* ('tooth'), and the owner of the animal is only liable to pay for this type of damage when done in a private field, not when done in the public domain (based on Exodus 22:4, 'and it feed in *another man's field*'). Nevertheless, the *mishnah* rules, even though the owner of the animal is not obliged to pay the full value of the food consumed by the animal, he is obliged to pay for the benefit he has received in that he has been spared the cost of feeding the animal. Say, for instance, the food eaten is costly and worth five *zuzim* whereas the cost of the animal's meal is only half a *zuz*, the owner of the animal certainly is not liable to pay five *zuzim*, since there is no payment for *shen* in a public domain, but he is obliged to pay half a *zuz* since he has benefited to this amount.

Our *sugya* opens (20a end) with R. Hisda (end of third century) remarking to Rami bar Hama that if he had been in his vicinity on the previous day he would have heard a discussion on an interesting topic.[1] 'What was the interesting topic?' asks Rami, to which R. Hisda replies, it was the question whether one who resides on his neighbour's premises without his knowledge is obliged to pay rent.[2] That is to say, A occupies vacant premises belonging to B without asking B's permission and hence without any contract. The question is whether B can later demand that A pay him rent for the period in which he had resided on the premises. There is no question that B can evict A whenever he wishes but where he did not, perhaps because he was unaware of it at the time, does A, when he has eventually been evicted or when he has left the premises on his own accord, have to pay rent for the benefit he has enjoyed by living on the premises?

There is now an (editorial) elaboration of the problem. If A had other premises he could have occupied and B had no intention of renting out the premises, content to leave them vacant, it is obvious that in this case A has no obligation to pay rent for his occupation. This is a case of 'one has no benefit, the other no loss' (*zeh lo neheneh ve-zeh lo ḥaser*), and the question of compensation does not arise. If, on the other hand, B was anxious to obtain a rent-paying tenant for the premises and A had no other accommodation available to him, A obviously is obliged to pay the rent to B since this is the case of 'one has benefit, the other loss' (*zeh neheneh ve-zeh ḥaser*). In both these instances there is no problem, i.e. where there is neither gain to one nor loss to the other there is no question that there is no compensation, and where there is both gain to one and loss to the other there is no question that compensation must be made. The problem arises where A has benefited from the occupation, since he had no other premises he could have occupied, but B was content to leave the premises vacant and so has suffered no loss through A's occupation (*zeh neheneh ve-zeh lo ḥaser*). This is R. Hisda's problem. Can A say to B, 'What loss have I caused you?' (i.e. and, consequently, there is no liability for rent), or can B retort, 'But you have benefited' (i.e. and there is a liability for rent).[3]

Rami says to R. Hisda, 'The solution to your problem is to be found in a *mishnah*.' 'Which *mishnah*?' R. Hisda asks. Rami replies, 'I shall tell you when you have performed some service for me,' whereupon R. Hisda took Rami's scarf and folded it for him.[4] The *mishnah* to which Rami refers is the *mishnah* to which the *sugya* is appended; the *mishnah* which states that the owner of the animal that ate food in the public domain has to pay the cost of the meal he would otherwise have had to give his animal. This shows that even where there is no loss to one, the other has to pay if he benefited.[5]

Rava, hearing of the discussion between R. Hisda and Rami, remarked, 'How little does a man whom God helps have to worry', i.e. Rami got away with a faulty analogy without receiving any protest from R. Hisda. There is no comparison between the *mishnah* and our problem, since in the case mentioned in the *mishnah* there is loss to the owner of the food. But, the Talmud asks, what will Rami say to this? — i.e. surely Rami must have noticed that there is no analogy at all between the two cases. To this the reply is given that in the normal way anyone who leaves food in the public domain has abandoned it. Consequently, the loss cannot be taken into account (once the food has been abandoned it is no longer his, so that the animal has not caused him the loss but his having left the food there in the first instance), and the payment stated in the *mishnah* can only be for the benefit the owner of the animal has received. This proves that where 'one benefits and the other suffers no loss' there is a liability to pay.[6]

The Talmud now proceeds to try and solve the problem from another *mishnah* (*Bava Batra* 1:3). Here the following case is discussed. A has a field surrounded on all four sides by fields belonging to B. B fences round three sides of A's field and here, the *mishnah* states, A is not obliged to contribute to the cost of the fencing since his field is still open on the fourth side and the fencing is of no benefit to him. From this it can be inferred that if B fenced round all four sides of A's field, so that A too, benefits from the fencing, A is obliged to contribute to the cost of the fencing. Now in this case B has suffered no loss by benefiting A since he has done the fencing to protect his own fields, and yet A is liable to make a contribution. This shows that where there is no loss to one but benefit to the other there is liability. No, replies the Talmud, in this case B does suffer a loss through A because of the extra outside fencing required to encompass A's field in the middle.

The Talmud now turns to the ruling of R. Jose in the same *mishnah*. R. Jose states that if A himself fenced round on the fourth side, he thereby demonstrates that he wishes to have his field fenced round and he is consequently liable to contribute towards the cost of the other three walls. The implication of this is that if B fenced round the fourth side, A would not be liable even though he benefits from the fencing. This shows that where one benefits and the other suffers no loss, there is no liability. And (Tosafists) it will not do to say that this is only the opinion of R. Jose since the Sages, who take issue with R. Jose, only do so because, as above, they hold that B does suffer a loss because of the extra fencing required. The Talmud replies that here A does not gain since, so far as he is concerned there is no need for a wall, only for a very cheap fence worth a *zuz* to act as a barrier. Thus there is no proof from the opinion of the Sages that A is liable to pay the rent, since the Sages may hold that in their case there is a loss to B. Conversely, there is no proof from the opinion of R. Jose that A is liable to pay the rent, since R. Jose may hold that in his case there is no real benefit to A.

The Talmud proceeds to try to solve the problem from another *mishnah* (*Bava Metzia'* 10:3). A owns the top storey in a house and B the ground floor. The whole structure falls in and A requests B to rebuild the ground floor so that A can then rebuild his top storey, but B refuses. The Sages rule that A can rebuild the ground floor and live there until B repays him for the costs A has incurred. Now it is implied that B does not deduct the rent that seems to be his due, which shows that, in fact, A is not liable to pay the rent since, although he has benefited, B has suffered no loss, B being unwilling to rebuild. This demonstrates that where one benefits and the other suffers no loss, there is no liability. No, replies the Talmud, the reason why A is entitled to live on the ground floor without paying rent is not because of the principle of benefit to one and no loss to the other, but rather because A's original ownership of the upper storey gives him a right to have a ground floor upon which the upper storey can be built. In other words he owes B no rent, because until he can live in the upper storey, the ground floor belongs to him and he is not enjoying any benefit from B.

The Talmud now turns to the opinion of R. Judah in this same *mishnah*. R. Judah holds that B can deduct the rent when he reimburses A for his outgoings. This can only be because one who benefits and the other suffers no loss is liable. (And, again, the Sages would have agreed with R. Judah were it not that, in their opinion, as above, A has a right to live on the ground floor.) The Talmud replies that there is no proof since this *mishnah* deals with a new house that is built and when B does eventually reimburse A for his outgoings, the walls of the house have been blackened through A cooking there and the like. Hence B does suffer a loss, albeit a very small one, and there is no analogy with the case of one who benefits and the other suffers *no* loss. Thus there is no proof from the Sages that in our case A does not have to pay rent, since in their case A has a right to live there free of charge. Nor is there any proof from R. Judah that in our case A does have to pay rent, since in his case there is a loss to B.

The Talmud now goes on to say that the problem was 'sent,' i.e. from Babylon, to R. Ammi, i.e. the Palestinian teacher. R. Ammi sent back the reply; What has he done to him? What loss has he caused him? What harm has he done to him? — i.e. why should A have to pay since B has suffered no loss. But when the problem was presented to R. Hiyya bar Abba he replied, the matter requires

further consideration, and when they sent to inquire a second time
R. Hiyya bar Abba replied, 'Why do you persist in bothering me?
If I had found the solution would I not have informed you?'

The Talmud now introduces a debate on the matter between two
Palestinian Amoraim, with the usual opening of debates in the
Talmud, *itmar*, 'It was taught.' These two teachers are R. Kahana
and R. Abbahu each purporting to give the true opinion on the matter
of their teacher, R. Johanan. According to R. Kahana, R. Johanan
ruled that A does not have to pay the rent, but according to R.
Abbahu, R. Johanan held that A does have to pay the rent. The later
Babylonian teacher, R. Pappa, observed that in fact R. Abbahu had
not heard any explicit statement from R. Johanan, but had drawn
the conclusion that this was R. Johanan's view because R. Johanan
had remained silent when he, R. Abbahu, had suggested that this
was the rule. All this, according to R. Pappa, took place when R.
Abbahu commented on yet another *mishnah* (*Me'ilah* 5:4). Here
it is stated that if a stone or a beam belonging to the Temple was
placed in a house and the person who placed it there enjoyed the
shade provided, that man is obliged to bring a trespass-offering in
atonement for the act of sacrilege. On this the Babylonian teacher,
Samuel, commented that the reference is to a man placing the beam
or the stone on the open roof even if he did not actually secure it
to the building (otherwise he would be liable even if he enjoyed no
benefit from it; the act of fixing itself constituting an act of sacrilege).
On this R. Abbahu commented in R. Johanan's presence, that this
shows that one who resides in his neighbour's house without in-
forming him does have to pay the rent, i.e. since the Temple has
suffered no loss from the man's enjoyment of the shade provided
by the beam or the stone. R. Johanan remained silent, from which
R. Abbahu drew the conclusion that R. Johanan concurred with his
deduction. But, observes the Talmud, in fact, R. Johanan's silence
was because he thought R. Abbahu's conclusion was so faulty that
he did not bother even to correct it. This is because Rabbah has said
that, 'so far as the Temple is concerned, lack of knowledge is equal
to knowledge in the case of a commoner,' i.e. (Tosafists) God always
knows when a trespass has been committed and the law of trespass
has nothing to do with the case of a human being residing in
someone else's house.[7]

The Talmud now continues to the effect that R. Abbahu bar
Zabda sent the following message to Mari bar Mar: 'Please ask

R. Huna for his opinion in our case.' But R. Huna had departed this life in the meantime so the reply was given by R. Huna's son, Rabbah, who declared: 'My father said in the name of Rav: A does not have to pay rent to B and if one rents a house from Reuben he has to pay the rent to Simeon.' On this the Talmud asks: What has Simeon to do with the matter? Rabbah son of R. Huna's comment is consequently amended to read: 'If one rents a house from Reuben and it is later found that the house belongs not to Reuben but to Simeon, he has to pay rent to Simeon.' But, objects the Talmud, Rabbah has said that no rent has to be paid at all? The answer is that the second clause, that the rent has to be paid, refers to the case where Simeon is concerned to rent out his house and here, of course, rent has to be paid since there is loss to the owner.

A similar set of observations now follows. R. Hiyya bar Abin said that Rav said, while others say, R. Hiyya bar Abin said that R. Huna said:'A does not have to pay rent to B. And if one rents a house from townsfolk he has to pay the rent to the owner.' The Talmud objects: What has the owner to do with it? — i.e. the townsfolk are the owners. Again the statement is amended to read: 'If it turns out that the townsfolk are not the owners, the rent has to be paid to the rightful owner.' But this contradicts the first statement, that no rent is to be paid? Again the answer is that the owner is concerned with renting out his house.

There now follows a new departure in the consideration of the question. R. Sehorah said that R. Huna said that Rav said: 'A does not have to pay rent to B since Scripture says, *Through Sheiyyah the gate gets smitten* (Isaiah 24:12)', i.e. the demon *Sheiyyah* goes to work on an uninhabited house and brings it to ruin.[8] That is to say, it is not only A who benefits by occupying the house. B also benefits in that the occupation of the house by A prevents it falling into ruins. Mar bar R. Ashi observes that he had himself seen such a demon and it gored like an ox (or, possibly, the meaning is that he had seen a house left uninhabited and it looked as if a wild ox had been let loose there). R. Joseph gives a slightly different reason why B benefits. This is because an inhabited house is kept in good repair, i.e. A benefits B as well as himself because, as a result of his occupation, the house is kept in good repair. The Talmud asks: What is the practical difference between the two reasons, that of *Sheiyyah* and that of keeping it in good repair? The difference is where B, although he had left the house vacant, still kept there his timber and straw. Here the demon has no foothold in any event since B visits the house from time to time. But the other reason does still apply. What the Talmud appears to be saying at this stage of the argument is, granted that in principle there has to be payment where one benefits and the other suffers no loss, this principle does not apply where the one benefits and the other not only suffers no loss, but himself benefits. The two benefits cancel one another out, so to speak.

The *sugya* concludes with a case decided by R. Nahman. A man built a villa on waste land belonging to orphans. R. Nahman took the villa from him in order to compensate the orphans. The Talmud assumes, at this stage, that the orphans had no use for the piece of land so the Talmud asks: Does this mean that R. Nahman holds that in our case A has to pay rent? No, replies the Talmud, some Carmoneans (a tribe of nomads) were in the habit of making use of the site and they would pay a small sum regularly to the orphans for the right to make use of the site. Thus it was a case of A benefiting and B suffering a loss. Strictly speaking all that R. Nahman was entitled to do was to force the man to pay rent for the use of the land on which he built the villa. And, in fact, this is what R. Nahman tried, at first, to arrange. But the man refused to heed R. Nahman's ruling so R. Nahman confiscated the villa.[9]

The *sugya* is structured as follows:

1 Discussion by R. Hisda and Rami — editorial analysis of when the problem arises — Rami's proof from *mishnah* and Rava's refutation.

2 Attempted proof from *mishnah*, *Bava Batra*, that A is liable: no proof because there is loss due to extension of walls.
Attempted proof from R. Jose that A is not liable: no proof because he does not need a proper wall.

3 Attempted proof from *mishnah*, *Bava Metzia'*, that A is not liable: no proof because A has right to ground floor.
Attempted proof from R. Judah that A is liable: no proof because there loss due to darkening of the walls.

4 R. Ammi: A is not liable.
R. Hiyya bar Abba: uncertain.

5 R. Kahana: R. Johanan ruled: A is not liable.
R. Abbahu: R. Johanan ruled: A is liable.
R. Pappa: R. Kahana ruled only indirect from Samuel and *mishnah*, *Me'ilah*.
No proof since trespass-offering is in different category.

6 R. Abba bar Zabdi, Mari R. Huna, Rabbah son of R. Huna,
  R. Huna in name of Rav: A is not liable.
  R. Hiyya bar Abba in name of Rav or R. Huna: A is not
  liable.
7 R. Sehorah in name of R. Huna in name of Rav: A is not
  liable a because of *Sheiyyah*; b because of good repair.
  Difference between a and b where previously house used for
  timber and straw.
8 R. Nahman's ruling: is it because he holds A is liable? No,
  there the orphans suffered loss.

If we look carefully at the above schematic arrangement it becomes
clear beyond doubt that we have here, as in most Talmudic *sugyot*,
an ordered, contrived progression of thought as part of a complete
literary unit, even though the material has been taken from different
periods and different climes (Rav and R. Johanan in the early third
century down to Mar son of R. Ashi in the second half of the fifth
century, to say nothing of the quotes from the Mishnah which are
even earlier). Thus the discussion between R. Hisda and Rami is made
to open the *sugya*, even though, as it appears later on, the matter
had been discussed as early as Rav and R. Johanan, because Rami
seeks to prove his case from the *mishnah* in *Bava Kama* to which
the *sugya* is appended. Moreover, in this *mishnah* the word *hanaah*
occurs and the issue is one of 'benefit' (*hanaah*). Sections 2 and 3
are presented in this order, even though *Bava Metzia'* precedes *Bava
Batra* in the Mishnah, because the refutation of the proof in section
2, that B suffers a loss, does not apply to the *Bava Batra* case and
hence it as if the Talmud is saying: Very well you have coped with
section 2 but how will you cope with section 3? And the pattern
in sections 2 and 3 repeats itself round the Sages and R. Jose and
the Sages and R. Judah. Suddenly, in section 7, a completely new
idea is introduced, that B gains because of *Sheiyyah* or because of
keeping the house in good repair. On this view, normally, there is
no case of the one benefiting and the other suffering no loss and
where there is, as in the case of the use for timber according to one
version, there would be a liability to pay. It follows that now we
have three cases: a this one benefits and this one suffers loss
                 b this one benefits and this one suffers no loss
                 c this one benefits and this one also benefits
This last case is kept in the background, as it were, because if it were

63

introduced earlier on in the *sugya*, it would have been difficult to discuss the cases of a and b. After the whole *sugya* has eventually arrived at the conclusion that A is not liable, R. Nahman's case is presented for discussion in that, on the surface, it seems to contradict the conclusion towards which the rest of the *sugya* has been leading. Thus the arrangement of the *sugya* abandons any chronological sequence in favour of a literary sequence in which, as in all good literary works, each part of the story is told at exactly the right moment.

6

Literary analysis of the *sugya* on taking the blame on oneself

The *sugya* in *Sanhedrin* 10b–11a provides an excellent illustration of how the editors of the Babylonian Talmud used earlier materials for the shaping of a complete and contrived literary unit. First, we must present the brief *sugya* in translation with explanatory notes in parenthesis, and then attempt to analyse its literary structure.

The *sugya* in translation

The Rabbis taught: The year can only be intercalated [by adding an extra month] by those who are invited for the purpose. [The Nasi, president of the Supreme Court, must invite, on the previous day, those who are to participate.] The story is told of Rabban Gamaliel[1] [the Nasi at the time] who declared: 'Arrange for me [lit. 'Let them rise early in the morning'] seven people to come to the upper storey' [where the procedure was to be carried out]. He arose on the morrow [lit. 'He arose early'] and found eight people there, whereupon he declared: 'Let the person who has come up here without permission [i.e. uninvited] go down again.'[2] Samuel ha-Katan[3] stood up, saying: 'I am the person who has come up without permission, but I have not come to intercalate the year but to learn a practical law which I required.' He [Rabban Gamaliel] said to him: 'Sit my son, sit; every year can suitably be intercalated through you but the Sages have said: The year can only be intercalated by those who are invited for the purpose' [i.e. and you, worthy though you are, have not been invited].

However, it was not Samuel ha-Katan [who had come up uninvited] but another person and he [Samuel] did it [to confess that he was the guilty one] in order not to embarrass the other.

As was the case when Rabbi [Judah the Prince] once sat and expounded but he sensed a smell of garlic, whereupon he declared: 'Let the person who has eaten garlic go away.' Rabbi Hiyya stood up and went out. Then [seeing that Rabbi Hiyya had gone out] they all stood up and went out. The next morning R. Simeon son of Rabbi met R. Hiyya and said to him: 'Are you the person who caused distress to my father?.' He said: 'That should never happen in Israel'[4] [i.e. Heaven forbid that I should be guilty of such a thing].

From where did R. Hiyya learn such conduct [to take the blame on himself even though he was not the guilty party]? For we have learnt: The story is told of a certain woman who came to the House of Study of R. Meir saying to him: 'Rabbi, one of you betrothed me by having intercourse with me.' R. Meir stood up, wrote a bill of divorce and gave it to her. Then they all stood up, wrote a bill of divorce and gave it to her.

From where did R. Meir learn such conduct? From Samuel ha-Katan. And from where did Samuel ha-Katan learn it? From Shecaniah the son of Jehiel, as it is written: *And Shecaniah son of Jehiel, one of the sons of Elam, answered and said unto Ezra: We have broken faith with our God, and have married foreign women of the peoples of the land; yet now there is hope for Israel concerning this thing* (Ezra 10:2).[5]

And from where did Shecaniah learn it? From Joshua, as it is written: *The Lord said unto Joshua, Get thee up, wherefore, now, art thou fallen upon thy face? Israel hath sinned* (Joshua 7:10–11).[6] Joshua said to God: 'Sovereign of the Universe! Who is the sinner?' He said to him: 'Am I an informer? Go and cast lots.'

And if you wish I can say, he [Shecaniah] learnt it from Moses, as it is written: *And the Lord said unto Moses: How long refuse ye to keep My commandments and My laws* (Exodus 16:28).[7]

Analysis of the *sugya*

The first section of the *sugya*, regarding Rabban Gamaliel and Samuel ha-Katan, is obviously a unit on its own. The purpose of the story is to support the statement that the year can only be intercalated by those who have been invited by the Nasi. This statement prefaces the story and is repeated by Rabban Gamaliel at the end of the story. The passage is Tannaitic, probably dating from the second century CE. This section is paralleled in the Jerusalem Talmud, *Sanhedrin* 1:2 (18c).

In the Jerusalem Talmud version there are a number of differences from that of the Babylonian Talmud. Here is the Jerusalem Talmud version: 'May associates [*haverim*, evidently here, young scholars who are not members of the Supreme Court] enter for the purpose of intercalating the year? We can resolve the question [lit. 'we can hear it'] from the story of Rabban Gamaliel who said: "Summon for me seven elders to the upper storey" [to intercalate the year] but eight came in. He said: "Who is it that has entered without permission?" Samuel ha-Katan stood upon his feet, saying: "It is I who has come up without permission. I required to know a decision in law [*halakhah*] and I came to ask about it." Said Rabban Gamaliel to him: "If even Eldad and Medad (Numbers 11:26–7) whom all Israel know to be two [suitable persons] I would still say that you are one of them" [i.e. you are certainly fit to intercalate the year]. For all that, they did not intercalate the year on that day, spending that day in debates on the Torah, and intercalating it on the next day.'

It would seem from the Jerusalem Talmud version that the problem with regard to Samuel ha-Katan was not because he had not been invited (there is no reference in the Jerusalem Talmud version to *mezumanim* as in the Babylonian Talmud), but because he was not a member of the Supreme Court, only a *ḥaver*. The story is quoted to show that *ḥaverim* can participate in the procedures. Rabban Gamaliel is annoyed that while he invited only seven, an additional, uninvited person had come up. Samuel ha-Katan admits that he is the uninvited person but he had no intention of 'gate-crashing', only that he had happened to be there for the purpose of asking an *halakhic* question, having nothing to do with the intercalation of the year.[8] It would thus seem that the purpose of the story in the Babylonian Talmud version is to prove that only invited persons can participate, while the purpose in the Jerusalem Talmud version is to prove that even *ḥaverim* can participate.

In any event, according to both versions, the Rabban Gamaliel story is a complete unit in itself and is limited to the theme of intercalation. In neither version is there any suggestion that it was not Samuel ha-Katan who was guilty but someone else. This motif of taking the blame on oneself for something of which one is not guilty is not found at all in the Jerusalem Talmud and in the Babylonian Talmud is obviously editorial and Amoraic. In other words, the editors of the Babylonian Talmud have used the story of Samuel ha-Katan because it can be adapted easily to the taking-blame motif, since here is a story about someone who confessed that he was the guilty party when the identification of that party was unknown. In the original Tannaitic source there is not the slightest suggestion that it was someone else who was the guilty party. That is the suggestion of the editors of the Babylonian Talmud for the purpose of developing their theme. Consequently, the attempt that has been made of identifying the real culprit is misguided.[9] In the original story there was only one culprit, Samuel ha-Katan.

The stories of R. Hiyya and R. Meir are found only here and are in Hebrew, unlike the general framework of the *sugya* which is in Aramaic. This would seem to support the view that the editors had before them the three stories (in Hebrew), of Samuel ha-Katan, of R. Hiyya and of R. Meir, the last two of which they left as they had received it, the first they adapted by postulating that it was not Samuel ha-Katan. However, the mere fact that it is in Hebrew does not prove that it is Tannaitic. From the comparison of the Jerusalem Talmud version with that of the Babylonian Talmud, it would seem that the Hebrew of the Samuel ha-Katan story is 'artificial,' i.e. the editors knew the story but gave it their own wording (which differs from that of the Jerusalem Talmud), and if this is so it may well be that the other stories, too, have been invented for the purpose of the taking of blame theme.

Something of the following seems to have happened. The editors of our *sugya* knew the story of Samuel ha-Katan and this was appended (as in the Jerusalem Talmud version) to the *mishnah* at the beginning of tractate *Sanhedrin*, in which it is stated that a court is required for the intercalation of the year. But this story was easily adaptable to the taking-of-blame theme by postulating that Samuel ha-Katan had confessed to a sin of which he was not guilty. This motif is then given prominence by quoting the other tales and thus leading back from generation to generation — from R. Hiyya through to R. Meir through to Samuel ha-Katan, through to Shecaniah and then to Joshua and Moses.[10]

The unusual attempt to make each one 'learn' the practice from a higher authority is to be explained on the grounds of the apparent dubiousness of the practice. It could have been argued that it was wrong for an innocent person to plead guilty in order to avoid causing the guilty party any embarassment. Against the practice, it can be argued, is the need to expose the guilty; to avoid the telling of lies; to prevent any misunderstanding by the authority who was offended. Against this can be set the abhorrence of sensitive persons of 'sneaking' on others and the idea, which seems implicit in the Shecaniah and the Moses proofs, of collective responsibility, i.e. everyone is really guilty when this kind of thing happens. Consequently, the theme is presented as if each one does not dare to take the responsibility of following this line of conduct without finding someone sufficiently close to him who can be relied upon to validate that course since he followed it himself.[11]

It must finally be noted that there follows on our *sugya*, stories about inspiration. That Samuel ha-Katan features in one of these provides the link with our *sugya*.[12] The editors, having digressed with the blame-taking motif, now revert to the original story of Samuel ha-Katan and add a further instance of the high regard in which he was held.

7

Literary analysis of the *sugya* of 'half and half'

According to the *mishnah* (*Ḥullin* 2:1), a valid act of *sheḥitah* for an animal involves the cutting through of the two organs, the food-pipe and the windpipe, and for a bird the cutting through of either one of these. However, the *mishnah* states, it is not necessary to cut the organ right through but it suffices if the greater part has been cut through. But if only half has been cut through in the case of a bird or only one and a half in the case of an animal, the *sheḥitah* is invalid.

The Talmudic *sugya* (*Ḥullin* 28b–29a), appended to this *mishnah*, opens with a debate between the third-century Babylonian Amoraim, Rav and R. Kahana, concerning 'half and half' (*meḥatzah 'al meḥatzah*), i.e. (at this stage of the discussion) where the *sheḥitah* cut was through only half the organ, half remaining as it was without any cutting. Rav said that half and half is counted as 'the greater part,' while R. Kahana said that half and half is not counted as the greater part. This receives the following (editorial) analysis. According to Rav, the law given to Moses regarding *sheḥitah* was: 'Do not leave the greater part of the organ without *sheḥitah*.' But according to R. Kahana the law was rather: 'Cut through the greater part.' The meaning[1] presumably is that, according to Rav, there is no rule that for the act of *sheḥitah* to be valid the greater part must be cut through. The demand for the greater part to be cut through is not a positive rule. It is intended only to negate the leaving of the greater part uncut, for then there is no act of *sheḥitah* at all, any more than there would be where a very small incision had been made. But according to Rav Kahana, there is a positive rule for the greater part to be cut through. It follows that where an exact half had been cut through, the *sheḥitah* is valid according to Rav, invalid according to Rav Kahana.[2]

A number of proofs are now adduced. The first of these is from our *mishnah*, in which it is stated quite explicitly that the *sheḥitah* is invalid where only half the organ has been cut through, and this clearly refutes the opinion of Rav. To this the reply is given that strictly speaking the *shehitah* is valid, as stated by Rav, where only half had been cut through. When the *mishnah* rules that the *shehitah* is invalid it is only as a Rabbinic rule, the Rabbis refusing to permit such a *shehitah*, valid though it is in itself, lest a man may imagine that he has cut through half the organ when in reality he has not cut through even half. Thus the requirement in the *mishnah* for the greater part to be cut through is only a precautionary measure. It is easy to detect the difference between cutting through the greater part and cutting through less than half, and here no precautionary measure is required. It is extremely difficult to detect the difference between exactly half and less than an exact half and so a precautionary measure is required. Thus, it is now suggested, when Rav ruled that half and half is counted as the greater part, he does not mean that the *shehitah* is completely valid, only that it is valid in itself. But, as the *mishnah* states, it is invalid by Rabbinic law. As *Rashi* observes, the bird or animal may not be eaten, by Rabbinic law, but, since the *shehitah* is valid *per se*, the bird or animal would not be a source of ritual contamination (the precautionary measure being limited to the prohibition of eating the bird or the animal). According to Rav Kahana this makes sense since, in his view, half valid *per se* by Biblical law and the bird or animal would be capable of affording ritual contamination.[3]

Rav Katina now quotes a *baraita* dealing with an earthenware oven that had become contaminated. It remains in the state of contamination until it has been broken into pieces (Leviticus 11:35). The *baraita* states that if the oven had been broken into two equal pieces, it remains in a state of contamination 'since it is impossible to be exact,' i.e. there will always be a doubt whether or not the two halves are exactly equal. One may be slightly larger than the other and, so far as that section is concerned, the oven is still intact, i.e. it has not been broken into pieces. Thus one of the pieces (the smaller) is now clean, but the other (the larger) remains unclean, and since we cannot determine which is the larger and which is the smaller they are both unclean because of doubt. The implication of the *baraita* is that if it were possible to have two equal halves, the oven would be clean. According to Rav Kahana this makes sense since, on his view, half is not treated as the greater part. But according to Rav where there are two equal halves, each is treated as the greater part and both halves such be unclean. The reply is given by R. Pappa, 'You cannot have two greater parts of the same object,' i.e. here Rav would agree that half is treated as half not as the greater part, since one cannot have two 'greater parts' in the same object. In the case of *shehitah*, on the other hand (as *Rashi* comments), we have no concern with the uncut part of the organ, and the fact that it remains uncut is of no relevance to the act of *shehitah* which, according to Rav, only requires half to be cut through. That is to say, in the case of *shehitah*, we are not concerned at all about the status of the half that has not been cut through. But in the case of the oven both halves have the same status, and it is illogical to treat either half as the greater part so as to treat it as the unbroken section of the oven.[4]

A third attempted proof is now advanced. A *baraita* is quoted in which it is stated that if a man cut through half the windpipe and then paused for the time it takes to perform the act of *shehitah*, and then he completed the *shehitah*, it is valid. Now there is to be no pause during the act of *shehitah*, otherwise the *shehitah* is invalid. Why then does the *baraita* state that when he completed the act of *shehitah*, afterwards it is valid? It can only be because the cutting through of half the windpipe is not considered to be part of the act of *shehitah*, so that when he completes the act afterwards it is as if he had performed the act of *shehitah* on a half-severed windpipe. But the rule is that an animal with a windpipe that has been severed in its greater part is forbidden (*terefah*) and, according to Rav, half is treated as if it were the greater part. To this the reply is given that the *baraita* is not speaking of *shehitah* of an animal, but of a bird. Here when the half of the windpipe had been cut through it is in any event permitted, since for a bird only one of the organs requires to be severed. Thus if half is treated as the greater part, a valid act of *shehitah* has been carried out and the pause is not a pause in *shehitah* at all. If, on the other hand, half is not treated as the greater part then, since only half of the windpipe has been cut through, the bird is not rendered *terefah* thereby.

A proof is now attempted from another *baraita*. Here it is stated explicitly that if *shehitah* is peformed on a bird, the *shehitah* is valid even if all that was done was to cut a windpipe that had been half severed, i.e. the man simply made a slight cut so that then the greater part of the windpipe had been severed. But why, according to Rav, is the bird permitted since, in his view, it is as if the greater part of the windpipe had been severed before *shehitah*? That is to say, in the previously quoted *baraita shehitah* had been carried out, but in this *baraita* the reference is clear that the half had been severed before the final cut. To this Rava replies that Rav will agree that in the case of *terefah* half is not treated as the greater part since, Rav agrees, for the severance to render the bird *terefah* 'a greater part that can be seen with the eye' is required. To this Abbaye objects that it is illogical to require a discernible greater part in the case of *terefah* and only half (treated as a greater part) in the case of *shehitah*. Abbeye's point is that some forms of *terefah* involve only a slight perforation; the perforation of the foodpipe, for instance, renders the bird or animal *terefah* even if it is exceedingly small. If then, argues Abbaye, even in the case of *terefah* where the greater part is required, for the bird or animal to be *terefah* in the instance of the foodpipe, *a fortiori* in the case of *shehitah* a discernible 'greater part' should be required. This seems to clinch the argument and refute Rav.

Yes, the Talmud now states, Rav agrees, in fact, with Rav Kahana: half is not treated as the greater part in connection with *shehitah* (i.e. and the formulation with which the *sugya* opens is mistaken). The debate between Rav and Rav Kahana concerns the law of the Paschal lamb. The law is that when a man is unable to bring the Paschal lamb because he is unclean on the eve of Passover, he brings a substitute on the second Passover (Numbers 9:1–14). But if the majority of the congregation are unclean, the law is that the Paschal lamb is offered up in the proper time, the obligation to bring the Paschal lamb setting aside the law against offering in an unclean state. What is the law where exactly half the community is unclean and the other half clean? This is debated by Rav and Rav Kahana. Rav here says that half is treated as the greater number. Consequently, each half is treated, so far as itself is concerned, as a majority and the clean half offers up the sacrifice in a state of cleanness, the unclean half in a state of uncleanness, both at the proper time. Rav Kahana disagrees, holding that here, too, half is not treated as a greater part. Consequently, the members of the unclean half are treated not as a community, but as individuals and they observe the substitute Passover.[5]

The *sugya* concludes that the reason why Rav holds that in the case of the Paschal lamb, half is treated as the greater number (while in all other cases he does not) is because here Scripture says, *If any man of you shall be unclean by reason of a dead body* (Numbers 11:10), in connection with the substitute Passover. From this verse we learn that only an individual is pushed away to the second Passover but not a community. Thus here, even though the half does not count as the greater part, yet neither does it count as 'any man,' as an individual.

The *sugya* is, then, structured as follows. The debate between Rav and Rav Kahana is recorded and explained. From the (editorial) explanation it emerges that the debate concerns *shehitah*. The first proof follows from the *mishnah* and the idea of Rabbinic precautionary measure introduced. The second proof, adduced by Rav Katina, is from the oven divided into two equal halves to which the reply is given by R. Pappa. The third proof is from the case of pausing and this is easily refuted. But this leads to the fourth proof. From the *baraita* it clearly emerges that the severance of only half the windpipe does not render the bird *terefah*. Rava replies that Rav will agree in the case of *terefah*. But Abbaye objects that it is an *a fortiori* argument. Hence, we must conclude, Rav and Rav Kahana were not thinking at all of *shehitah* and the debate is about the Paschal lamb.

The first thing we notice from the whole *sugya* is that in essence the debate between Rav and Rav Kahana is not about *shehitah* in particular, but about the general question of whether half and half qualifies as the greater part, otherwise what is the point of trying to prove the case from the oven and from *terefah*, and why is the same formulation used in these and the Paschal lamb instance. The idea behind the *sugya* is that where, in a given case, there is a reference to 'the greater part,' does this mean a positive greater part or does it mean that there is not to be a greater part of the opposite. The puzzling feature of the whole *sugya* is that until the end it is assumed that the original debate between Rav and Rav Kahana did concern *shehitah*, the instances of the oven and *terefah* being adduced by analogy. Thus not only the editorial elaboration, but the observations of R. Pappa, Rav Katina, Rava and Abbaye make the assumption that the original debate was in the case of *shehitah*.

All this can be explained in two ways:
1 The whole of the *sugya*, with the exception of the reversal at the end, was an original *sugya* with regard to *shehitah* upon which there was a second stage of redaction.
2 The whole *sugya* is an artificial construction, consciously arranged with misleading information for the sake of dramatic effect.

The second hypothesis becomes the more plausible once it is seen that the argument is developed in stages in which there is a constant play on when and when not can half and half be considered as the greater part. In other words, we have another example among many in the Babylonian Talmud of a contrived *sugya*.

8

Rabbi Joshua b. Hananiah and the elders of the house of Athens

The famous Talmudic tale of R. Joshua ben Hananiah and the 'elders of the house of Athens'[1] has been discussed at length by the traditional Talmudic commentators[2] and by modern scholars.[3] This chapter seeks to subject the story to literary analysis with a view possibly of shedding some further light on the general literary style and method of the Babylonian Talmud. The story is found in the Babylonian Talmud, tractate *Bekhorot* 8b–9a. Although the reference to R. Joshua and the gestation of a serpent is found in the *midrash*[4] and one or two of the riddles are found in another *midrash*,[5] the story in its entirety is only found in this section of the Babylonian Talmud.

The story begins with the question Caesar puts to R. Joshua, 'What is the duration of a serpent's gestation and birth?,' to which R. Joshua replies, 'Seven years.' But, Caesar objects, the 'elders of the house of Athens' coupled a male serpent with a female and she gave birth after no more than three years, to which R. Joshua replies that at the time of the coupling the female had already been pregnant for four years. That cannot be, argues Caesar, since a pregnant animal does not copulate. R. Joshua replies that serpents, like human beings, do copulate even when the female is pregnant. But, objects Caesar, this casts doubts on the wisdom of the Athenian Sages, to which R. Joshua replies that 'we,' i.e. the Jewish Sages, have greater wisdom than the Athenians. This leads Caesar to propose that R. Joshua should proceed to the Athenians and engage them in intellectual contest and, if R. Joshua wins the contest, he should bring the Athenians to Caesar. R. Joshua agrees. He asks Caesar how many Athenian Sages there are and he is told that they are sixty in number. He requests Caesar to provide him with a ship containing sixty compartments with sixty thrones[6] in each compartment. Caesar provides the ship according to R. Joshua's specifications and R. Joshua sets sail on his mission.

R. Joshua b. Hananiah and the elders of the house of Athens

On his arrival, R. Joshua proceeds to the slaughter-house where he finds a man dressing an animal. He asks the man the price of a head and he is told that it is half a *zuz*. R. Joshua pays the half *zuz* and then declares he did not say that it is the head of the animal that he wanted but the head of the man himself (i.e. presumably he wanted the man to be his slave). R. Joshua declares that he will release the man provided that he points out to him the residence of the Athenians. The man is afraid to obey since the Athenians kill anyone who discloses their secret residence. R. Joshua advises the man to take a bundle of sticks and, when he arrives at the residence, to pretend to rest (i.e. and R. Joshua will follow him from afar). Following his plan, R. Joshua arrives at the secret residence.

The Athenians had stationed guards[7] outside the entrance and inside in such a way that if, on examination, they saw footprints facing inwards this would show that the outside guards had let an unauthorised person in, and if they saw footprints facing outwards this would show that one of the elders had left without authorisation. The guards who let unauthorised persons in or out were slain by the elders. R. Joshua turned his shoes so that the footprints faced both ways and both sets of guards were slain, enabling R. Joshua to get in. (We are not told how R. Joshua managed to elude the guards in order to make the two sets of footprints. Presumably, the meaning is that he did this while the guards were walking round the compound on their tour of inspection so that the entrance was clear for a short while).[8]

R. Joshua is now within where he sees that the Athenians in session have a peculiar arrangement, the younger but wiser men being seated higher than the older but less wise men. R. Joshua is thus faced with a dilemma. If he greets those in the higher position the older men will be affronted, but if he greets the older men the younger will be affronted. R. Joshua resolves to extend a greeting that will embrace both younger and older: 'Greetings to all the Sages.' The Athenians ask R. Joshua what he wants and he tells them that he has come to learn of their wisdom: 'I am the Sage of the Jews[9] and I wish to learn of your wisdom.' Ask away, declare the Athenians, but R. Joshua proposes that they engage in a contest. If they win they can do with him as they please, but if he wins they must agree to break bread with him in his ship. The Athenians agree and the contest begins.

There now follows a series of riddles put by the Athenians to each of which R. Joshua supplies the right answer: The first question is: A man wanted to marry a woman but her family refused to allow the match. Why would this man then try to marry a woman of a higher social class than the first (i.e. since he was unsuccessful in his first attempt with a woman of lower rank)? R. Joshua replies by taking a peg and trying to hammer it into the wall without success. He then takes the peg and hammers it into the wall at a higher point and he is successful in hammering it in (i.e. the key to success after a failure is not to aim lower but higher).[10]

Second question: A man borrowed money and was unable to repay with the result that his land was taken from him in payment of the debt. Why would such a man borrow again? R. Joshua replies: 'A man goes into the forest to cut wood but finds he is unable to carry the logs into the town because they are too heavy. He cuts more wood in the hope that someone will see his predicament and help him carry the whole burden' (i.e. better luck next time[11] and people will feel sorry for him).

The Athenians now say: Tell us some tall stories.[12] R. Joshua replies: 'A mule once gave birth and a bond was found around the neck of its offspring in which it was stated: "Someone has a claim on my father's house to the tune of a hundred thousand *zuz*." ' But, objected the Athenians, a mule cannot give birth. 'There you have your tall story', replied R. Joshua.

The Athenians now put this question to R. Joshua: When salt has lost its savour how can it be salted? 'With the after-birth of a mule', replied R. Joshua. Can a mule have an after-birth? 'Can salt lose its savour?' (i.e. ask a silly question and you will get a silly answer).

The Athenians now request R. Joshua to build them a house in the sky. R. Joshua, through the magical use of a divine name, suspends himself in mid-air and requests the Athenians to bring him there the bricks and mortar required for the building of the house. How is this possible? How is it possible to build a house in the sky?

Now the Athenians ask R. Joshua to show them where the earth's centre is situated. 'Right here,' replies R. Joshua, pointing with his finger. How do we know that you are right? 'Bring ropes and measure it.'

We have a well in the field, say the Athenians, bring it for us into the town. R. Joshua replies: 'Make for me ropes of bran flour and I shall pull it into the town.' Our millstone is broken, please sew it together again. R. Joshua declares: 'Extract from it a thread as the weavers do and I shall use it to sew up the millstone.'

A further question now follows. How does one reap a furrow of knives? 'With the horn of an ass.' But does an ass have horns? 'Can there be any such thing as a furrow of knives?'

The Athenians now bring R. Joshua two eggs and ask him to tell them which comes from a white hen and which from a black. R. Joshua brings to them two cheeses and asks them to tell him which comes from a white goat and which from a black.

A further question: When a chick dies whence does its spirit depart? 'From where the spirit entered thence does it depart.'

Show us an article to buy which is not worth the trouble it causes. R. Joshua buys a huge mat of reeds which is too big to get through the door unless the door is first demolished. 'There you have an article that is more trouble than it is worth.'

R. Joshua, having won the contest, takes the Athenians to the ship, placing each one in a separate compartment. Each one, seeing the sixty thrones in his compartment, imagines that the others will soon come there (i.e. so they sit there without protest and the ship can set sail without their knowledge). Before leaving the shore R. Joshua takes some soil with him in the ship. When the ship reaches the place that swallows,[13] he fills a jug with the water of that place.

Arriving at Caesar's palace the Athenians are seen to be in a state of distress so that Caesar cannot believe that these are the renowned Athenian Sages. R. Joshua scatters some of their native soil over them and this restores their balance, upon which they address Caesar in a disrespectful manner so he tells R. Joshua to do with them as he pleases. R. Joshua puts the water he had taken from the sea into a pail and he orders the Athenians to fill the pail with water. The more water they pour into the pail, the more the water is swallowed up. The shoulders of the Athenians become dislocated through their efforts and they perish.

First it must be noted that this story occurs here in tractate *Bekhorot*, because the section immediately preceding it deals with the duration of the gestation period for serpents and other animals. It is possible the story is an interpolation, i.e. after the tractate has been redacted,[14] but even if it belongs to the original redaction process it forms a separate unit with only a very loose association with the rest of the *sugya*. This unit, in its present form, is obviously very late. It is in Aramaic and in the style of the Babylonian Talmud.[15] The genre is that found among all cultures of the apparently weak folk-hero getting the better of the more powerful representatives of the enemies of his people, as in the David and Goliath story. Unlike the stories of Moses' confrontation with the Egyptian sorcerors and Elijah's confrontation with the prophets of Baal, the contest between R. Joshua and the Athenians is conducted on the natural level. With the exception of the episode in which R. Joshua elevates himself skywards by means of the divine name (and that is really incidental to R. Joshua's victory),[16] the Jewish Sage wins through his superior intellectual prowess, naturally so since the whole purpose of the tale is to demonstrate that Jewish *wisdom* is superior to the *wisdom* of the vaunted Athenians. R. Joshua plays fair throughout, defeating the Athenians at their own game. The role of Caesar in the story must not be overlooked. It is implied that while the Jews know of their own superiority, the Gentile ruling power is also compelled, albeit reluctantly, to acknowledge that superiority.

Fairy-tale though our story is, it is a fairy-tale told (at least in the form we now have it) by scholars in the usual style of such stories in the Babylonian Talmud, witness the tales of the 'Jewish Sinbad the Sailor', Rabbah bar bar Hanah.[17] To see it, as some do, as in any way contemporaneous with R. Joshua is to miss the point entirely. R. Joshua is the hero of 'his' tale, just as Rabbah bar bar Hannah is the hero of 'his' tales.[18]

The tale seems to follow a definite pattern:

1 The stage is set.
2 R. Joshua arrives.
3 R. Joshua gains entrance.
4 R. Joshua introduces himself.
5 The contest proceeds.
6 The ship is boarded and sets sail.
7 They all arrive and the Athenians perish.

It might be reading too much into the narrative to see this as a conscious use of the 'sacred' number seven,[19] but it is just possible that this numbered sequence is part of the pattern.

In the light of the above, the traditional commentators, who read into the narrative various philosophical and theological ideas, are far off the mark,[20] though it is just possible that the impossible birth stories and the question of the salt without savour are anti-Christological.[21]

9

Bavli and *Yerushalmi* on Rabban Gamaliel and Rabbi Joshua

There are two versions of the narrative about Rabban Gamaliel being deposed. One of these is in the Babylonian Talmud (*Berakhot* 27b–28a); the other in the Jerusalem Talmud (*Berakhot* 4:1, 7c–b), with a parallel in the Jerusalem Talmud (*Ta 'anit* 4:1, 67d). First the two versions are given in translation and then compared.

The Babylonian Talmud version

Our Rabbis taught: The story is told of a certain disciple who came to ask R. Joshua whether the Evening Prayer is optional or obligatory. 'It is optional,' he replied. When the disciple asked Rabban Gamaliel the same question, he replied: 'It is obligatory.' 'But,' said he, 'R. Joshua told me that it is optional.' He [Rabban Gamaliel] said to him: 'Wait till the shield-bearers[1] enter the House of Study.' When the shield-bearers had entered the House of Study, the questioner rose to his feet and asked: 'Is the Evening Prayer optional or obligatory?' 'It is obligatory,' said Rabban Gamaliel, who then asked of the Sages: 'Does anyone dispute this ruling?' 'No,' said R. Joshua. 'But it was told to me in your name that it is optional?' said he. R. Joshua replied: 'If I were alive and he dead, the living could refute the dead. But since I am alive and he is alive, how can the living refute the living?'

So Rabban Gamaliel sat there expounding while R. Joshua remained on his feet till all the people began to murmur and they said to Hutzpit the *turgeman*:[2] 'Stop,' and he stopped. They said: 'For how long can he [Rabban Gamaliel] go on insulting him [R. Joshua]? Last year, on *Rosh ha-Shanah*, he insulted him. In the matter of Rabbi Zadok, in *Bekhorot*, he insulted him.[3] And now he again insults him. Let us depose him. And whom shall we appoint to his stead? Shall we appoint R. Joshua? He is the one involved. Shall we appoint R. Akiba? Rabban Gamaliel may punish him [by his supernatural powers] since he does not enjoy ancestral merit [to shield him from Rabban Gamaliel's punishment]. Let us appoint R. Eleazar b. Azariah for he is wise, he is rich and he is tenth in line from Ezra.' 'He is wise', so if questions are presented he will be able to cope with them.'He is rich', so if the Emperor needs to be served [i.e. if a gift has to be given to appease the Roman authorities], he can afford it. 'And he is tenth in line from Ezra', so his ancestral merit can shield him from Rabban Gamaliel's displeasure.

They came to him [to R. Eleazar b. Azariah] saying: 'Is the Master willing to assume the office of Head of the *metivta*?'[4] He replied: 'I must take counsel with my wife.' He went to take counsel with his wife who said: 'They may depose you' [as they deposed Rabban Gamaliel]. He replied: 'It is worthwhile to use a valuable cup[5] for a single day even if it is broken the next day.' 'But,' she said, 'you have no white hair.' He was [only] eighteen years of age but a miracle occurred and eighteen rows of his hair turned white. This is why R. Eleazar said,[6] 'Behold I am *like unto one who is* seventy years of age', and he did not say, [simply] 'I am seventy years of age'.

It was taught: On that day the guard was removed from his post and permission was granted for [all] the disciples to enter [the House of Study]. For Rabban Gamaliel had caused a proclamation to be issued stating: 'No insincere disciple [lit. 'one whose inside is not like his outside'] may enter the House of Study.' On that day many benches were added [to accommodate the increase of disciples]. R. Johanan said: 'The matter is debated by Abba Joseph b. Dosethai and the Sages; according to one opinion four hundred benches were added, according to the other opinion seven hundred benches were added.' Rabban Gamaliel was distressed, saying: 'Heaven forfend, perhaps I have prevented Israel from studying the Torah.' They showed him in a dream white casks filled with ashes. But this dream had no significance and its purpose was solely to set Rabban Gamaliel's mind at rest.

It was taught: *Edduyot*[7] was taught on that day and wherever the expression is used 'on that day' it refers to this day. And there remained no law the doubts concerning which were unresolved in the House of Study. Rabban Gamaliel himself did not absent himself from the House of Study. For we have learnt:[8] On that day Judah, the Ammonite proselyte, came before them in the House of Study. He asked them: 'Am I permitted to enter the congregation? [to marry a Jewish woman]. Rabban Gamaliel said: 'You are forbidden to enter the congregation.' R. Joshua said: 'You are permitted to enter the congregation.' Rabban Gamaliel said to him [to R. Joshua]: 'Does it not say: *An Ammonite or a Moabite shall not enter into the congregation of the Lord* (Deuteronomy 23:4)?' R. Joshua replied: 'Do Ammon and Moab still reside in their original home? Sennacherib King of Assyria had long ago gone up and mixed up all the nations, as it is said: *I have removed the bounds of the peoples and have robbed their treasures and have brought down as one mighty their habitations* (Isaiah 10:13). And whatever is separated it is from the majority that it is separated.[9] Rabban Gamaliel said to him: 'But have they not returned? For the verse states: *But afterwards I will bring back the captivity of the children of Ammon, saith the Lord* (Jeremiah 49:6).' R. Joshua replied: 'Is it not said: *And I will turn the captivity of My people Israel* (Amos 9:14) and they have still not returned?' So they permitted him to enter the congregation.

Said Rabban Gamaliel: 'Then I must go and appease R. Joshua.' When he arrived at his house he noticed that the walls were blackened. Said he:

'I see from the walls of your house that you are a smith.' Said he: 'Woe to the generation of which you are the leader for you have no idea of how hard the scholars have to struggle in order to earn their living.' 'I humble myself before you. Please forgive me', he said, but he took no notice until he said, 'Do it for the sake of my father's house', and he then allowed himself to be appeased.

They said: 'Who will go and tell the Rabbis?' 'I will go,' said a certain laundryman. R. Joshua sent this message to the House of Study: 'Let the one who is accustomed to wearing the robe wear it. But shall one unaccustomed to wearing the robe say to one so accustomed, remove your robe and I shall wear it?' Said R. Akiba: 'Close the door lest Rabban Gamaliel's servants come in to cause distress to the Rabbis.' So R. Joshua said: 'It is better if I go myself.' He went there, knocked on the door and said: 'Let the sprinkler [of purifying water] son of a sprinkler sprinkle. But shall one who is neither a sprinkler nor the son of a sprinkler say to a sprinkler son of a sprinkler, your water is cave water and your ashes oven ashes?'[10] R. Akiba said: 'Joshua, we only did it all on your behalf and since you have been appeased so be it. Tomorrow we shall both rise early to go to his door.[11]

Then they said: 'What shall we do now? Shall we depose him [R. Eleazar b. Azariah]? We have a tradition that there can be ascent but no descent in sacred matters.[12] If we allow one Master to preach on one Sabbath and the other on the next Sabbath, this will result in jealousy. Let, therefore, Rabban Gamaliel preach on three Sabbaths and R. Eleazar b. Azariah on the fourth. And it is with reference to this that the Master says:[13] "Whose Sabbath was it? It was the Sabbath of R. Eleazar b. Azariah." '

And that disciple was R. Simeon b. Yohai.

The Jerusalem Talmud version

And the story is told of a certain disciple who came and asked R. Joshua: 'What is [the status of] of the Evening Prayer?' 'It is optional,' he replied. He asked Rabban Gamaliel but he replied: 'It is obligatory.' Said he: 'Tomorrow at the Meeting House (*bet ha-va 'ad*) rise and ask what the law is in this matter.' So on the morrow the disciple rose and asked Rabban Gamaliel: 'What is the Evening Prayer?' 'It is obligatory,' he replied. Said he: 'But R. Joshua has told me that it is optional?' Said Rabban Gamaliel to R. Joshua: 'Do you say it is optional?' 'No,' he replied. Said he: 'Rise to your feet that they may testify against you.' So Rabban Gamaliel sat there expounding while R. Joshua remained standing till all the people murmured and said to Hutzpit the *turgeman*: 'Dismiss the people.' Then they said to R. Zinon, the official (*hazan*), 'Begin to recite', and he began to recite: '*For upon whom hath not thy wickedness passed continually?*' (Nahum 3:19).

So they went and appointed R. Eleazar b. Azariah to the *yeshivah*.[14] He was only sixteen years old, yet his whole head became full of grey hair. R. Akiba sat there in distress, saying: 'It is not that he: [R. Eleazar b.

Azariah] is a greater son of the Torah [i.e. more learned] than I, but he is a son of great men and I am not. Happy the man whose ancestors bring merit to him. Happy the man who has a peg upon which to hang.' Of what did this peg of R. Eleazar b. Azariah consist? He was tenth in line from Ezra.

And how many benches were there? R. Jacob b. Sisi said: 'There were eighty benches of scholars (*talmidey ḥakhamim*) apart from those who stood behind the barrier.' R. Jose b. Avun said: 'There were 300 benches apart from those who stood behind the barrier.'

As we have learnt:[15] On the day they appointed R. Eleazar b. Azariah to the *yehivah*. We learn there:[16] R.Eleazar expounded this in the presence of the Sages in the vineyard at Jabneh. Was there a vineyard there? But this refers to the scholars who sat in rows like vines in a vineyard.

There and then Rabban Gamaliel made his way to each and every one of them to appease him. When he came to R. Joshua he found him sitting and manufacturing needles. He said: 'From these you earn a living?' Said he: 'And until now you did not want to know. Woe to the generation of which you are the leader.' Said he: 'I humble myself before you.'

So they sent a laundryman[17] to R. Eleazar b. Azariah. Some say it was R. Akiba [whom they sent]. He said to him [to R. Eleazar b. Azariah]: 'He who is a sprinkler the son of a sprinkler let him sprinkle. He who is neither a sprinkler nor the son of a sprinkler, should he say to a sprinkler the son of a sprinkler, your water is cave water and your ashes ashes of the oven?' Said [R. Eleazar b. Azariah]: 'If you have been reconciled, let you and I rise up early to Rabban Gamaliel's door.' Nevertheless, they did not depose him [R. Eleazar b. Azariah] entirely but they appointed him Head of the Court.

Analysis

Thus the two versions tell the same story, the major part in identical words. Both versions seem to be using a common source each elaborating on this in its own way. Behind the story there appears to be echoes of the struggle between the Princely House and the rest of the Sages, a struggle mentioned not infrequently in the Talmudic literature.

The main features common to both versions are: Rabban Gamaliel's insulting behaviour to R. Joshua for which he was deposed; Rabbi Eleazar b. Azariah's appointment in his stead; the increase of the benches; the reconciliation; the saying about 'the sprinkler'; R. Joshua's 'Woe unto the generation'. There are, however, differences between the two versions. In the Babylonian Talmud we are provided, as the 'punch-line' to the story, with the name of the disciple whose question began it all. In the Jerusalem Talmud the disciple remains anonymous. In the Babylonian Talmud the scholars tell Hutzpit to stop in his translation. In the Jerusalem Talmud they tell him to dismiss the school. In the Babylonian Talmud there is no mention of R. Zinon the *hazan* or his declaration against Rabban Gamaliel. On the other hand, the Jerusalem Talmud makes no reference to the other occasions on which Rabban Gamaliel insulted R. Joshua. In the Babylonian Talmud there is considerable deliberation before they appoint R. Eleazar b. Azariah, the candidatures of R. Joshua and R. Akiba being first proposed and then rejected. In the Jerusalem Talmud R. Eleazar b. Azariah is appointed without ado. There is nothing in the Jerusalem Talmud of R. Eleazar b. Azariah consulting his wife. In both versions R. Eleazar b. Azariah's hair turns white (or grey), but in the Jerusalem Talmud version the phenomenon is not ascribed to a miracle. In the Jerusalem Talmud R. Eleazar b. Azariah is only sixteen; in the Babylonian Talmud he is eighteen. In the Jerusalem Talmud there is nothing explicit about the guard at the door, and it is possible that in the Jerusalem Talmud the benches were simply added because there was an influx of new disciples because of the new regime. There is nothing in the Babylonian Talmud of 'those who stood behind the barrier'. There is reference to a debate regarding the number of benches that were added in both versions but both the amounts and the name of the disputants differ. In the Babylonian Talmud R. Johanan states that the dispute is between Abba b. Dosethai and the Sages, while in the Jerusalem version the dispute is between R. Jacob b. Sisi and R. Jose b. Avun. In the Babylonian Talmud the number of benches is either 400 or 700, while in the Jerusalem Talmud it is either eighty or 300. The number 300 is not uncommon for a large number, but the significance of the other numbers is obscure. The whole episode of the further debate, on the Ammonite proselyte, between Rabban Gamaliel and R. Joshua is missing from the Babylonian version. And there is no reference in the Jerusalem Talmud to '*Edduyot*' being taught on 'that day'. In the Jerusalem Talmud Rabban Gamaliel goes to appease 'each and every one'. In the Babylonian Talmud he goes only to R. Joshua. In the Jerusalem Talmud R. Akiba takes an important part, according to 'some', in the reconciliation. In the Babylonian Talmud R. Akiba is, at first, determined to resist it. In the Babylonian Talmud it is the Sages who refer to R. Eleazar's ancestral merit. In the Jerusalem Talmud it is R. Akiba. In the Jerusalem Talmud R. Joshua yields immediately to Rabban Gamaliel's entreaties. In the Babylonian he only does so after Rabban Gamaliel has appealed to his father's house. There is no reference in the Jerusalem Talmud to the saying about wearing the robe. In the final reconciliation in the Babylonian Talmud, R. Eleazar b. Azariah retains his elevated position but preaches on only one of the four Sabbaths in the month. In the Jerusalem Talmud he is appointed to a different position, that of Head of the Court.

It can be seen that the Babylonian version is not only more elaborate, but it is more dramatic. Typically of the Babylonian Talmud, the material is arranged so that the story unfolds gradually in true literary style in which nothing is disclosed until the appropriate moment.

10

Bavli and Yerushalmi on Rabbi Dosa and the Sages

There are two versions of the narrative about R. Dosa b. Harkinas and the Sages; one in the Babylonian Talmud (*Yevamot* 16a), the other in the Jerusalem Talmud (*Yevamot* 1:6, 3a–b). It may be fruitful to compare the two versions.

The law discussed in the narrative concerns levirate marriage. There are two brothers A and B. A has two wives X and Y and X is B's daughter. A dies without issue. Now the law is clear that B cannot perform levirate marriage with X since she is his daughter, but can he carry out the duty with Y? According to the House of Hillel, just as there is no levirate marriage with X there is none with Y, the 'rival of his daughter' — *tzarat ha-bat*. (And since there is no obligation Y is forbidden to B as his brother's wife.) But according to the House of Shammai, a 'rival of a daughter' is permitted (and there is, consequently, the obligation of levirate marriage).[1]

We can now examine the two versions in English translation.[2]

The Babylonian Talmud version

In the days of R. Dosa b. Harkinas the rival of the daughter was permitted to the brothers [of the deceased]. This ruling was disturbing to the Sages since he [R. Dosa] was a great Sage. But his eyes were dim and he was unable to attend the sessions in the House of Learning. So they said: 'Who shall go to consult with him?' Said R. Joshua: 'I will go.' 'And after him?' 'R. Eleazar b. Azariah.' 'And after him?' 'R. Akiba.'

They went to him and waited at the entrance to his house. His maidservant went in and said to him: 'The Sages of Israel have come to visit you. 'Let them come in', he said, and they came in. He took hold of R. Joshua and seated him on a golden couch. 'Master,' said R. Joshua, 'please allow your other disciple to be seated.' 'Who is he?' 'R. Eleazar b. Azariah.' 'Has our friend Azariah a son?' declared the Master and he applied to him the verse: *I have been young and now I am old; yet I have not seen the righteous forsaken, nor his seed begging bread* (Psalms 37:25). So he took hold of R. Eleazar b. Azariah and seated him, too, on a golden couch. 'Master,' said R. Joshua, 'please let your other disciple be seated.' 'Who is he?' 'Akiba b. Joseph.' 'You are', said he, 'Akiba b. Joseph, whose name is known from one end of the world to the other. Be seated my son, be seated. May there be many like you in Israel.'

They then discussed many topics with him[3] until they arrived at the topic of the rival of the daughter. 'What is the ruling regarding the rival of a daughter?' they asked him. 'This question is debated,' he replied, 'by the Houses of Hillel and Shammai.' 'And which ruling is followed?' 'The ruling of the House of Hillel'[that the daughter's rival is forbidden], he replied. But they said: 'It has been reported in your name that the ruling follows the House of Shammai.' He asked them: 'Did you hear this in the name of Dosa or in the name of the son of Harkinas?' They replied: 'We heard it just as the son of Harkinas.' He said: 'I have a young brother, a first-born of Satan, whose name is Jonathan and he is a disciple of Shammai [and it must have been Jonathan who gave the ruling]. Take care that he does not get the better of you in legal argumentation for he has three hundred arguments[4] to demonstrate that the rival of a daughter is permitted. But I call heaven and earth to be my witness that on this very mortar[5] sat Haggai the Prophet and gave the following three rulings: that a daughter's rival is forbidden, that in the lands of Ammon and Moab the poor man's tithe is to be given in the Sabbatical Year,[6] and that proselytes may be accepted from the Cordyenians and the Tarmodites.'[7]

It was taught: When they came in they entered through one door but when they went out out they made their exit through three [different] doors. He [Jonathan] confronted R. Akiba with his arguments and left him standing [in confusion]. Said he: 'Are you Akiba b. Joseph whose name goes out from one end of the world to the other? Happy are you that you won such fame without having reached the stage of oxherds.'[8] 'Not even of shepherds,' replied R. Akiba.

The Jerusalem Talmud version

R. Jacob b. Idi said in the name of R. Joshua b. Levi: It once happened that the Elders came to R. Dosa b. Harkinas to ask him concerning the question of the daughter's rival. They said to him: 'Is it you who permits the daughter's rival?' He said: 'Did you hear it in the name of Dosa b. Harkinas?' 'We heard it in the name of the son of Harkinas,' they replied. He said: 'It was my brother, Jonathan, who is a first-born of Satan and he is one of the disciples of Shammai. Take care for he has three hundred arguments to permit the daughter's rival.'

They made their way to him [Jonathan] and he [Dosa] wrote [in a letter he gave to them to deliver]: 'Take care for the Sages of Israel are coming to see you.' They came in and sat before him. He presented his arguments to them but they did not grasp them. He explained them in greater detail and they still were unable to grasp them. They began to drop off to sleep. He said, 'How dare you fall asleep', and he began to throw pebbles at them. Some say that they came in through one door but made their exit through three [different] doors.

He [Jonathan] sent to him [Dosa]: 'You sent to me men who still require to study and you call them Sages of Israel.'

They came to him [Dosa] and they asked him for his opinion. He said: 'On this very mortar was seated Haggai the Prophet and he testified to three things: that the daughter's rival is permitted to marry [even] a priest; that in the lands of Ammon and Moab the poor man's tithe is to be given on the Sabbatical Year; and that proselytes may be accepted from the Tarmodites.'

He then said: 'Let me lift up mine eyes so that I can see the Sages of Israel.' When he saw R. Joshua he applied to him the verse: *Whom shall one teach knowledge* (Isaiah 28:9).[9] 'I recall,' said he, 'how his mother would take him in his cradle to the Synagogue so that his ears could cleave to words of the Torah' [from his infancy]. To R. Akiba he applied the verse: *Young lions do lack and suffer hunger* (Psalms 34:11).[10] 'I recognise him as a man mighty in the Torah.' When he saw R. Eleazar b. Azariah he applied to him the verse: *I have been young and now I am old* (Psalms 37:25). He said: 'I recognise him as in the tenth line from Ezra whom he resembles in appearance.'[11] R. Haninah of Sephoris said: 'R. Tarfon was also present there and he [Dosa] applied to him the same verse that he applied to R. Eleazar b. Azariah.'

Analysis

There are many strong points of resemblance in the two versions but there are equally strong points of difference. In both versions Dosa gives his ruling in the name of the Prophet Haggai while sitting on the mortar; in both Haggai testifies to the same three things; in both Dosa refers to his brother Jonathan as 'Satan's first-born'; in both Jonathan takes on the Sages and lives up to his reputation by scorning them; and in both Dosa quotes the verse in praise of R. Eleazar b. Azariah. While both versions agree on these matters, the actual formulation of some of the details is different.[12]

The major difference between the two versions is in the order of the Sages' visits. In the Babylonian Talmud they first arrive at the house of Dosa who gives them a royal welcome. He warns them of the skill of his brother in debate and they then meet with the brother.[13] In the Jerusalem Talmud version, Dosa sends them off to Jonathan at once, warning him beforehand in a letter. Jonathan gets the better of them and they return to Dosa who then welcomes them and states the contrary ruling of the Prophet Haggai.[14] The Babylonian Talmud version is stated anonymously;[15] the Jerusalem Talmud version in the name of R. Jacob b. Idi in the name of R. Joshua b. Levi.

How can the differences be explained? It is hard to tell, but a closer examination of the two texts shows clearly that the Babylonian Talmud version is the more dramatic. Thus in this version Dosa first gives the Sages confidence for their coming contest with Jonathan and, by praising R. Eleazar b. Azariah and R. Akiba, he is on their side right from the beginning. In the Jerusalem Talmud version, Dosa does not disclose his own view until they have been defeated by Jonathan. He lets them fight it out first. This is an illuminating example of the dramatic style of the Babylonian Talmud, concerned at least as much with the 'medium' as with the 'message.'[16]

11

The Rabbi Bannaah stories in
Bava Batra 58a–b

The passage we are considering is first given in translation.

Bava Batra 58a–b

R. Bannaah[1] used to mark caves [in which the dead had been buried, i.e. he used to mark the outlines of the caves on the surface so that people would avoid stepping over the graves and suffer ritual contamination, Numbers 19]. When he came to the cave in which Abraham was buried [the Cave of Machpelah], he found Eliezer, Abraham's servant, at the entrance, and he said to him: 'What is Abraham doing?' He replied: 'He is lying in the wings of Sarah [i.e. in her arms] and she is gazing at his head.' Said he: 'Go and tell him that Bannaah waits at the entrance.' Said he: [Abraham]: 'Let him enter. He knows full well that there is no *yetzer* ['inclination', i.e. no sexual desires] in that world.' He entered, gazed there [to take the measurements of the cave] and then went out. When he came to the cave of Adam [who was also buried there together with Eve but in a separate compartment], a *Bat Kol* ['Heavenly voice'] proclaimed: 'You have look-ed upon the resemblance of Mine image [the patriarch Jacob.][2] Do not look upon Mine image itself' [i.e. Adam, created in God's image, Genesis 1:29]. 'But I have to mark the cave.' 'The inner cave [in which Adam and Eve are buried] has the same measure as the outer cave' [in which Abraham and the other patriarchs and matriarchs are buried]. And according to the opinion that the two compartments were [not one behind the other on the same level but] one above the other [the *Bat Kol* said]: 'The measurements of the lower cave [in which Adam and Eve were buried] are the same as those of the upper cave' [in which the patriarchs were buried].

R. Bannaah said: 'I did manage to see his [Adam's] two heels and they appeared to be like orbs of the sun.'[3]

All [other human beings] in comparison with Sarah are like a monkey compared to a human being. Sarah compared with Eve is like a monkey compared with a human being. Eve compared with Adam is like a monkey compared with a human being. Adam compared with the *Shekhinah* is like a monkey compared with a human being.

The beauty of Rav Kahanah was only a [pale] reflection of the beauty of R. Abahu.[4] The beauty of R. Abahu was only a [pale] reflection of the beauty of Jacob our Father. The beauty of Jacob our Father was only a [pale] reflection of the beauty of Adam.

A certain Magus[5] used to dig up the dead.[6] When he came to the cave of R. Tobi b. Mattenah he [R. Tobi] seized hold of him. Abbaye came and said: 'Please let him go.' Another year he [the Magus] came again and this time he [R. Tobi] seized his beard. When Abbaye came he [R. Tobi] refused to let him go until he [Abbaye] brought scissors and cut off the beard [of the Magus].

A certain person declared [in his last will and testament]: 'A barrel of earth to one of my sons; a barrel of bones to one of my sons; and a barrel of feathers to one of my sons.' They did not know what he meant so they asked R. Bannaah. 'Have you land?' he asked them. 'Yes,' said they. 'Have you cattle?' 'Yes.' 'Have you cushions?' 'Yes.' 'Then that is what he meant.'[7]

A certain person overheard his wife saying to her daughter: 'Why are you not more cautious when you sin? This woman [herself] has ten sons and only one is from your father.' On his deathbed the man declared: 'All my property is to go to [only] one of my sons.' They did not know which of the sons he meant so they asked R. Bannaah. He said to them: 'Go and bang on your father's grave until he rises to tell you which one of you he left his estate.' They all went there to do it except for the one who was the real son. He did not go. So he [R. Bannaah] declared: 'All the estate belongs to that one.' They reported him to the government, saying, 'There is a certain man among the Jews who extracts money from people without witnesses and without any reason',[8] and they arrested him. His wife went to the prison and called out: 'I had a slave. They cut his head off, skinned him, ate his flesh, filled the skin with water and gave their companions[9] to drink but they gave me nothing for it.' They did not know what she meant so they asked R. Bannaah and he said: 'A goat skin bottle' [they killed her goat and made a bottle out of its skin]. They thereupon declared: 'Since he is so wise let him be appointed a judge.'

He [R. Bannaah] noticed an inscription over the gate which read: 'Any judge who is sued in court is no judge.' He said: 'In that case anyone can disqualify a judge by summoning him to court.' It should rather say: 'Any judge from whom money is taken justly by court is no judge' [i.e. if he has to be summoned to the court before he pays his debts, he is unscrupulous]. So they wrote: 'But the Jewish Sages say: Any judge who is summoned to court and money is justly taken from him is no judge.'

He saw another inscription which read: 'At the head of every death I, Blood, am there. At the head of all life I, Wine, am there.' 'But surely if a man falls from the roof and is killed, it is not Blood that kills him. And if a man is about to die, will he recover simply because he drinks Wine?' This is how it should read: 'At the head of all sickness I, Blood, am there. And at the head of all healing I, Wine, am there.' So they wrote: But the Jewish Sages say: 'At the head of all sickness I, Blood, am there. And at the head of all healing I, Wine, am there. Wherever Wine is available no other medicines are needed.'

Analysis

The passage has no parallels elsewhere except for the statement regarding the beauty of R. Kahana and the others which occurs in *Bava Metzia'* 84a. In that passage the great beauty (*shufra*)[10] of R. Johanan is praised and then the Talmud asks: But did not the Master say, 'The beauty of R. Kahana is only a [pale] reflection of the beauty of R. Abahu' and R. Johanan is not mentioned there?, to which the reply is given that, unlike the others, R. Johanan, though very handsome, did not have a beard. This does not necessarily mean that the editors of *Bava Metzia'* are quoting our passage in *Bava Batra*. 'But did not the Master say' may be to the statement itself which may originally have been unconnected with either passage.

The cross-reference to the two opinions on whether the two compartments in the Cave of Machpelah were one within the other or one on top of the other is to *'Eruvin* 53a where the matter is debated, though here, too, the reference may be to the debate itself not necessarily to the passage in *'Eruvin*.[11]

The whole passage, in its present form, is a unit on its own, but is obviously connected with the previous passage in *Bava Batra* (57b) in which there are some sayings attributed to R. Johanan in the name of R. Bannaah, the hero of our passage.

Although now a unit, our passage appears to have been the result of amalgamating two originally distinct units: (1) R. Bannaah and the cave (to which the tale of the Magnus has been added as appropriate to the theme of reverence for the dead saints); and (2) the tales about R. Bannaah's wise decisions. This second motif is similar to that in the tale (*Bekhorot* 8b–9a) of R. Joshua b. Hananiah getting the better of the Athenian Sages. In both the aim is to demonstrate the superior wisdom of the Jewish Sages.[12] In both passages the term 'the Sage of the Jews' is used, here of R. Bannaah, there of R. Joshua.

The passage in its present form follows a clear pattern in which the stages are as follows:

1 R. Bannaah and the Cave of Machpelah. R. Bannaah, in the process of his investigation, manages to obtain a glimpse of the resplendent heels of Adam.

2 This leads to the saying about the beauty of Sarah and Eve, and so forth.

3 This, in turn, leads to the statement about the beauty of R. Kahana, and so forth.

4 The story of the Magus and R. Tobi is then introduced. This takes place in Babylon, but the connection with the story of R. Bannaah and the patriarchs is obvious.

5 R. Bannaah solves the puzzle in the wording of the will.

6 R. Bannaah solves the further riddle of the man with only one true son.

7 R. Bannaah is arrested and saves himself by solving the riddle suggested by his wife.

8 R. Bannaah is appointed as a judge and suggests alterations to the two inscriptions.

The relationship between the two sections (1–4 and 5–7) is not only because of R. Bannaah, but also because the second section is also about this saint and death. It is as if the editors are saying: R. Bannaah as a marker of graves had gained much expertise in matters arising when a death has taken place. In section 6, R. Bannaah actually advises them to behave undecorously at the grave in order to get at the truth just as, in section 1 R. Bannaah himself behaves indecorously by entering Abraham's cave since his motive is sound.

The passage about Abraham lying in Sarah's arms was a source of amazement to the medieval authors who generally tended to treat the story in allegorical fashion.[13] But there is no real warrant for refusing to understand the legend more or less literally. The folk motif of the saints being alive after their 'death' is well known in both Jewish and general folklore.[14]

12

The device of *addehakhi*, 'just then'

The following three *sugyot* in the Babylonian Talmud afford paticularly convincing evidence of how the material, *halakhic* as well as *aggadic*, has been structured by the editors so as to provide a strong element of dramatic effect.

Menaḥot 37a–b

The *sugya* opens with a problem Pelemo presented to Rabbi Judah the Prince (called generally simply 'Rabbi'): On which head does a two-headed man put on the *tefillin*? Rabbi replied: 'Either go in exile[1] [as a penance] or be subjected to the ban', i.e. Rabbi suspected Pelemo was mocking him by presenting a nonsensical problem since there are no two-headed men.[2] At that moment (*addehakhi*) a man came along and said: 'An infant with two heads has been born to me. How many *shekalim* am I obliged to give to the priest for the redemption of the first-born?' That is to say, five *shekalim* is the usual amount for the redemption of the first-born (Numbers 18:16) and here, since the infant has two heads, perhaps ten *shekalim* are required, one for each head. An old man (*ha-hu sava*) taught that he must give the priest ten *shekalim*. Is that so? asks the Talmud. Did not Rami b. Hama teach: 'Since the verse says: *The first-born of man thou shalt surely redeem* (Numbers 18:15), I might have concluded that this applies even when the first-born became a *terefah*.[3] Scripture therefore states *Howbeit* (*akh*) to limit it'? (i.e. Scripture excludes from redemption a child who became unviable — *terefah* — and since a child with two heads is a *terefah*, no redemption at all is required). To this the Talmud replies that the case of the two-headed infant is different since Scripture states that the redemption is *per head* (Numbers 3:47), i.e. so that although the two-headed infant is a *terefah* each of the *heads* requires its own redemption.[4]

In this *sugya* Pelemo first sets his hypothetical problem, which

Rabbi considers to be insulting. Pelemo is vindicated, however, by the man who comes to ask his question just at the right moment. The old man quotes a *baraita* which similarly supports Pelemo by implication. But, the Talmud objects, there is the *baraita* quoted by Rami b. Hama and the reply to this is given.

The *dramatis personae* in the story are Rabbi, Pelemo, the old man and Rami b. Hama. The quote from the latter is not peculiar to our *sugya* and is found elsewhere[5] in the Babylonian Talmud. Rabbi is, of course, an historical figure, but it by no means follows that the incident with Pelemo is historical. Pelemo is mentioned elsewhere in the Babylonian (but never in the Palestinian) Talmud,[6] but only here in connection with Rabbi. In one passage Pelemo takes on Satan.[7] This does not allow us to conclude that Pelemo is a fictitious character, but it does tend to cast doubts on the historical nature of the narrative in our *sugya*. 'That old man' in the Talmud has been identified with Elijah, but the Tosafists[8] point to at least one passage where such an identification is impossible. It is worth noting, nonetheless, that, like Elijah, this mysterious person is often introduced as coming forward just at the precise moment when he is needed.[9]

In the narrative, both 'that old man' and the man whose wife had given birth to a two-headed child come in at exactly the right moment, as in a play or a novel when a character makes his entrance at exactly the right moment. The expression *addehakhi*, used for the entrance of the man with the query about the infant, is found in a number of instances in the Talmud, largely with the meaning of 'just then.'[10]

Ketubot 67b

This narrative is part of a *sugya* dealing with a poor man's claim for relief from the charity-chest or from private individuals. The section opens with the account of a poor man who requested Rava to support him. When Rava asked the man to tell him the kind of meals to which he was accustomed, the man replied that he was in the habit of eating fat chicken and drinking old wine. Rava protested that the man ought to be less extravagant in his tastes, instead of requiring the community to cater to his luxurious style of living. To this the man replied: 'Do I consume that which belongs to them? I consume that which belongs to God.' The Talmud quotes in this connection the verse: *The eyes of all wait for Thee, and Thou givest their food in his due season* (Psalms 145-15). The verse speaks of '*his* season', not '*their* season', to teach that each person has his own individual needs and it is God who sees that these are satisfied. Just then (*addehakhi*) there arrived Rava's sister, whom he had not seen for thirteen years, and she brought him some fat chicken and old wine. Rava held that the coincidence was teaching him something, and he admitted that he had spoken out of turn when he rebuked the man. Here the dramatic element in the tale is obvious. Note particularly the statement that Rava had not been visited by his sister for thirteen years. When she did arrive at Rava's house after all those years, she just happened to bring as a present the very food the poor man claimed he was entitled to enjoy!

Yevamot 105b

The *sugya* is appended to the *mishnah* (12:4) in which it is stated that *halitzah* performed by a sister-in-law who is a minor is invalid. R. Judah states in the name of Samuel that this is the opinion of R. Meir but the Sages hold that it is valid. The Talmud identifies 'the Sages' with R. Jose on the basis of a story about this Sage from which it emerges that he holds this view.

The story tells of Rabbi's son, R. Simeon, and R. Hiyya who were getting ready to enter the House of Learning to hear the exposition that Rabbi would shortly deliver. As they were waiting they discussed[11] whether the worshipper's eyes should be directed towards the Sanctuary on earth (i.e. the Temple in Jerusalem) or towards the Sanctuary on high, (i.e. the Heavenly Temple). Each quoted a Scriptural verse in support of his view. Just then (*addehakhi*)[12] R. Ishmael son of R. Jose came along and he asked them what they were debating. He reported that his father, R. Jose, had ruled that the worshipper's eyes should be directed downwards, but his heart should be directed upwards. Just then (*addehakhi*) Rabbi entered to deliver his discourse and the scholars went to take their seats. R. Hiyya and R. Simeon were young and nimble and were able to go quickly to their allotted places. But R. Ishmael, who was much older, had to proceed slowly and could only proceed to his place by stepping over the heads of the seated disciples.

Abdan,[13] disciple and attendant of Rabbi, cried out: 'Who is this who dares to step over the heads of the holy people,' R. Ishmael replied: 'I am Ishmael son of R. Jose and I have come here to learn Torah from Rabbi's mouth.' 'Are you worthy,' protested Abdan, 'to learn Torah from Rabbi's mouth?' 'Was Moses worthy to learn Torah from God's mouth?' R. Ishmael said. 'Are you Moses?' declared Abdan. 'Is your master God?' replied R. Ishmael. The Talmud records here that the third-century Amora, R. Joseph, commented on the episode that Rabbi received what he deserved (by allowing Abdan to insult R. Ishmael). For R. Ishmael referred to Rabbi as '*your* master' not as '*my* master.'

Just then (*addehakhi*) a sister-in-law presented herself to Rabbi (for the purpose of *ḥalitzah*). Rabbi instructed Abdan to have her examined to see if she possessed the signs of puberty (since if she were a minor the *ḥalitzah* would be invalid). As Abdan made his way out, R. Ishmael reported in the name of his father, R. Jose, that the *ḥalitzah* of a minor is valid, whereupon Rabbi called Abdan back, saying: 'The old man [R. Jose] has already rendered a decision.' As Abdan was returning from his aborted exercise, he was obliged to step over the heads of the seated disciples, whereupon R. Ishmael declared: 'He whom the holy people require may step over the heads of the holy people. But how dare one whom the holy people do not require step over the heads of the holy people.' 'Stay where you are,' the Rabbi ordered Abdan.

The passage concludes: 'It was taught: At that time (*be-oto sha 'ah*) Abdan became leprous, his sons were drowned and his two daughters-in-law made declarations of refusal' (*miun*).[14] The Talmud adds: R. Nahman b. Isaac said: 'Blessed be the All-merciful who put Abdan to shame in this world' (i.e. Abdan was punished in this life that he might enjoy eternal bliss in the Hereafter).

It is noteworthy how the whole narrative proceeds in dramatic form. R. Ishmael arrives just as the other two are discussing the question of prayer. This enables him to establish his authority as a reporter of his father's rulings. It also explains why he was prevented from taking his seat without having to step over the heads of the holy people. Rabbi arrives just at the right moment (for the purpose of the story) for Abdan to insult R. Ishmael. Again, just at the right moment, the sister-in-law arrives. To be noted, also, is the play on sisters-in-law in the story, the sister-in-law who arrives and the sisters-in-law who are Abdan's daughters-in-law. Perhaps the discussion of prayer is also intended to convey the idea that though R. Ishmael was obliged, as an old man who had to look where he was going, to look downwards and step over the heads of the disciples, his heart was directed Heavenwards and he had no intention of slighting them. In the whole episode, as well as in the story of Pelemo, there are probably echoes of the conflicts between the House of the Prince and the scholars.[15]

Conclusion

If the argument in the previous pages of this book is correct, and if the type of literary analysis it pursues is convincing, a number of conclusions can be drawn as to the nature of the Babylonian Talmud in its present form. First, it has been noted that the editors of the *Bavli* were not averse to putting some views into the mouths of earlier teachers where they had no tradition that these teachers really said what they are reported to have said. This was not done with any attempt to deceive, any more than the authors of acknowledged pseudepigraphic works intended to deceive their readers. Although the editors of the *Bavli* nowhere acknowledge the pseudepigraphic nature of the work, this is simply the result of their general silence on the question of what they were trying to achieve. With careful study of the material it can be seen that the editors used pseudepigraphy as one of the literary devices for the construction of the *sugya*. The purely academic nature of a good deal of the material can similarly be discerned by the cautious student.

The element of contrivance can also be discerned when a *sugya* is examined in the form in which it has been shaped by the editors. As we have tried to show, the typical Talmudic *sugya* is so arranged that the argument proceeds, in true dramatic fashion, so as to lead by stages to a climax. This element is, of course, present in all the Talmudic/*midrashic* works but, as a comparison with the same material in the *Yerushalmi* shows, nowhere so skilfully and intentionally as in the *Bavli* .

It is to this element of contrivance in particular to which this book has sought to draw attention. To repeat the Shakespeare illustration, a Shakespeare scholar, able to discover all the sources the great playwright used, would still be far off the mark in terms of understanding and appreciation if he imagined that Hamlet was not a play but a history of the Prince of Denmark. It never ceases to astonish me that so much work has been done by Talmudic scholars on the history and background of the Talmudic texts, and so little on the literary form to which the texts belong.

Of course, our hypothetical Shakespeare scholar does not exist. It is impossible to read Hamlet without seeing it for what it is. With regard to the Talmud, however, the element of contrivance and striving for dramatic effect is far from evident. On the whole, the Talmud is in prose form (with the exception of a few actual poems, eulogies, and the like), so that the particular form to which this book seeks to draw attention is elusive in the extreme. It is our contention that the final editors did their work so well that the work can be and has been studied by generations of keen students without any appreciation of this important feature. This is precisely what a skilful author does. He uses his stylistic methods to produce for his readers a work of enlightenment or entertainment or both, without admitting them into his secret. The skeleton is undoubtedly there, but the bare bones have been fleshed out.

It might not have been made too clear in the previous pages, but I am certainly not suggesting that the editors/authors of the Babylonian Talmud made it all up out of their own heads. Clearly they used much earlier material, including material, especially in the narrative portions, that had previously received some kind of literary, even dramatic, form. But, although they may well have used earlier material complete in itself, they re-worked this material, telling, so to speak, the old stories in a new way of their own. Nor do I suggest that they were interested in style for its own sake. Their chief interest, which they shared with those they hoped to educate, was in the knowledge of the Torah. Yet, evidently, they felt that such knowledge was best conveyed in a style that holds the reader's attention. Moreover, it has to be said, this style did not consist of the skilful use of language. The vocabulary of the Talmud is comparatively limited. It is dry, with few flourishes and even fewer elegant expressions. The attention of the student is held, rather, by bringing him into the House of Study of the Amoraim to participate in their debates and arguments. But, and this is the point, it is all presented in an exciting way, with each argument appearing at just the right moment, a way in which the debates and discussions themselves were surely not conducted. In other words, in the Babylonian Talmud, we do not have a *record* of what went on in the learned circles of the Amoraim, but a *story* of what went on or is supposed to have gone on and, as in any good story, the events have been rearranged and some of the details invented.

We can see how the editors/authors of the *Bavli* went to work from a careful analysis of the way almost every Talmudic *sugya* has been structured. Structured is the key word. The earlier material has not simply been thrown haphazardly together, nor has it been presented, as in the Mishnah or as in one of the Codes — that of Maimonides, for example — in a severely logical arrangement in which the rules follow a neat sequence. Rather, the details are introduced, as in a play or a novel, at the stage when they will make the greatest impact. This is quite obvious with regard to the material analysed in chapter 12 where, it has been shown, the term *addehakhi* means precisely 'just then' in the sense of just at the right moment. Neither is much analysis required in order to uncover the well-thought-out pattern of the material on the Biblical books discussed in chapter 3, where it is all arranged intentionally according to an 'ordered' sequence, since the theme itself is the *order* of the Biblical books. Attention has been called here, however, to the light the passage throws incidentally on how Rabbinic works, like the Babylonian Talmud, were compiled. A brief resume of chapters 4 to 11 will show us that the editors shaped their material even when this shaping is not immediately evident and has to be uncovered by cautious analysis.

Note how the editors set about their task of shaping the material discussed in chapter 4. Since the list of sayings by Ulla in the name of R. Eleazar appears in the Jerusalem Talmud, it is obvious that the *sugya* has been built around this list. Yet the material has been reworked and the discussion on it introduced in a symmetrical pattern. The theme of whether slaves are treated as real estate or as moveables, for instance, has been recorded at the end of the list (unlike in the Jerusalem Talmud version), so as to lead on to the elaborate discussion of this theme as virtually a *sugya* on its own, but with the closest association to the *sugya* on the original list. By no stretch of the imagination can all this be in the nature of a simple record of the debates and discussions as they actually took place. Similarly, in the *sugya* discussed in chapter 5, the actual ruling by the latest authorities is left until later because, after the whole analysis of 'this one benefiting and this one suffering no loss', it is then implied that, in reality, there is hardly such a case since in most cases both enjoy some benefit. It is not suggested that the whole episode of R. Hisda and Rami has been 'made up' out of the editors' heads. There probably was *some* discussion on the topic by these two teachers, but surely not in the contrived but highly effective way presented in the *sugya* as we now have it.

We have noted in chapter 6 that the story of Rabban Gamaliel and Samuel ha-Katan is found in both the Babylonian Talmud and the Jerusalem Talmud. It is hard to say whether these two passages suggest that the events actually happened, or whether they are two versions of an original fictitious tale of what happened. No doubt something of a similar nature really did take place in the time of Rabban Gamaliel, but the form in which the event is now recorded in both the Babylonian Talmud and the Jerusalem Talmud is the work of the editors. Moreover, the original account, which may well be Tannaitic, has obviously been reworked so as to provide the link with the quite different question of whether or not it is right for an innocent person to take the blame on himself. And this is peculiar to the *Bavli*.

The fictitious element is stated explicitly in the *sugya* discussed in chapter 7. The debate between Rav and R. Kahana is first presented in apparently circumstantial form, suggesting that an actual debate on *shehitah* took place between these two teachers, but, as the discussion proceeds, it is suggested that the debate was not about *shehitah* at all but about the totally different question of the Paschal lamb; the sole link with the *shehitah* question being the term 'half and half'. To ask why, if this is so, we were allowed to take the wrong direction in the first instance, is akin to asking why, in *The Merchant of Venice*, Shakespeare did not arrange for the leaden casket to be opened first or, to give a more banal illustration, why Goldilocks only ate the baby bear's porridge after she had tasted the porridge that was either too hot or too cold. In the police report of a murder investigation, the identity of the culprit would no doubt be stated at the beginning but if, in a detective story, the fact that the butler did it was disclosed in the first chapter, no one would wish to read the book.

It has been shown in chapter 8 that parallels to the story of R. Joshua and the elders of the house of Athens are found in the *midrashic* literature and are, in any event, typical of folk-tales in all cultures about 'one of us' getting the better of 'them'. Yet it is clear that the editors have reworked the material they probably had so as to turn it into a kind of scholarly diversion in which the arguments seem to matter far more than the tale itself, without the element of sheer story-telling being obscured. Once the material is recognised for what it is, the soundest warning is implicit that historians should exercise the greatest caution in using this and the stories treated in chapters 9, 10 and 11 for historical reconstruction of Rabbinic life in Rabbinic times. They may try to get at the facts behind the fiction, but that course is one notoriously fraught with difficulty.

The story about Rabban Gamaliel being deposed, treated in chapter 9, is in a category of its own in that the same story is told with much more circumstantial detail in almost identical words in both the *Bavli* and the *Yerushalmi*. Historians are not entitled, however, to reconstruct the event of Rabban Gamaliel's actual deposition since these two versions are stories depending, no doubt, on a common source but one that may be sheer fiction. To say this is not to deny that there is probably a historical, factual core to the narratives. It is clear, in any event, that the *Bavli* has reshaped the original material in its own typical, elaborate way, even though here the *Yerushalmi* has used a not dissimilar method.

The same applies to the material considered in chapter 10. Here, too, the same story is told in both the *Bavli* and the *Yerushalmi* with a good deal of the same circumstantial detail and in very similar words. The most convincing way of explaining this is that the details which occur in both versions — Haggai giving his three rulings while sitting on the mortar; the reference to Jonathan as 'Satan's first-born'; the argument in which Jonathan gets the better of the Sages and Dosa's praise of R. Eleazar b. Azariah — are not the work of the editors, but belong to the common source utilised by both the *Bavli* and the *Yerushalmi*, the *Bavli* developing or retelling the story in its own way, the *Yerushalmi* in its own way. With regard to this retelling in different ways by the *Bavli* and the *Yerushalmi* here, in the Rabban Gamaliel and in the many instances where the *Bavli* tells the story in one way, *Yerushalmi* the same story in a different way, it may be possible for an adventurous historian to discover that the different ways of telling the story are due, say, to different political and social conditions in Palestine and Babylon, but there would be a strong element of guesswork in the attempt. To repeat what has already been said, in considering such matters it is not only a question of whether the tradition supposed to be recorded is reliable, but whether it was intended in the first instance as the record of a reliable tradition.

Finally, with regard to the R. Bannaah material discussed in chapter 11, it is easy to see how folk-tales about a Palestinian hero have been adapted by the *Bavli* for its own purposes. Particularly to be noted is the way in which the Babylonian tale of R. Tobi and the Magus, and the cross-references to other statements, have been woven into the narrative. Sources have undoubtedly been drawn upon but recast to form a consecutive narrative.

As noted previously, David Halivni has coined the useful term Stammaim ('Anonymous Ones') for the editors who provided the framework of the *sugyot*, instead of the conventional division of the teachers into Tannaim, Amoraim and Saboraim. Halivni rightly prefers Tannaim, Amoraim, Stammaim and Saboraim. In the light of our investigation, it is necessary to go much further than Halivni to see the Stammaim as far more than mere editors of earlier material. They were, in fact, creative authors who shaped the material they had to hand to provide the new literary form evident in the passages we have examined and, indeed, on practically every page of the Babylonian Talmud.

Many of the details remain obscure, but something like the following happened to produce the Babylonian Talmud in the form and structure we now have of this gigantic work. The Amoraim in both Babylon and Palestine discussed the Mishnah and the other works of the Tannaitic period and they debated and discussed many other topics as well. The editors of the Babylonian Talmud, the Stammaim, used all this material in a fresh, creative way. These editors may have had before them, as a number of recent scholars have postulated, proto-*sugyot*, but these too have been restructured. Some of these proto-*sugyot* may have been left intact, the final editors doing what, according to the Documentary Hypothesis, 'R' did when incorporating into 'his' work 'J', 'E', 'D' and 'P'. Once the Babylonian Talmud had been restructured in this way, the Saboraim (and, possibly, here and there the early Geonim) made the comparatively few additions noted by the standard methodologies; the opening passages of tractates, *Kiddushin* and *Bava Metzia'*, for example, where the style, different from the rest of the Talmud, points to different redactional hands.

It remains to be said that if clear and numerous instances of literary device and contrivance can be detected in the Babylonian Talmud, it is hard to see how such a process can have resulted from a series of purely verbal forms of transmission. Since, as we have demonstrated, many such instances are indeed found, the most powerful support is given to the view of Maimonides in the Middle Ages and of the majority of modern scholars that the Babylonian Talmud emerged from the hands of its final editors in written form.

Glossary

Aggadah: lit. 'telling'; the non-legal material in the Talmud.

'am ha-aretz: lit. 'people of the land'; an ignoramus, opposite to *talmud hakham*, a scholar.

androginos: hermaphrodite.

Av Bet Din: head of the Court.

Bat Kol: 'a voice from Heaven'.

ba 'ya: academic problem.

Bavli: lit. 'of Babylon'; the Babylonian Talmud.

dina de-malkhuta dina: 'the law of the land is law', binding upon Jews.

ganav: sneak thief.

gazlan: robber.

Gemara: 'teaching'; another name for the Talmud.

Geonim: Post-Talmudic authorities in Babylon, seventh to tenth century.

get: bill of divorce.

gufa: lit. 'body'; of a text, the text itself.

hagigah: sacrifice offered on festivals.

hakhamim: Sages.

halakhah: Law, the legal material in the Talmud; also the actual ruling in a given case, corresponding to *hilketha* in Aramaic.

halitzah: lit. 'Drawing'; drawing off the shoe, the ceremony whereby a widow is released from the levirate bond.

hanaah: benefit, advantage.

hatihah de-issura: lit. 'forbidden piece'; where a man declares that something is forbidden on religious grounds, it becomes so for him though not for others.

hatzer: lit. 'courtyard', acquisition of objects when deposited in a person's domain.

haverim: 'associates', scholars.

hazan: from root 'to see', an overseer or official.

horaah: the rendering of a decision in Jewish law.

kal vahomer (pl. *kalin ve-hamurin*): argument from the minor to the major.

karka': land, real estate.

katzar: laundryman.

kinyan: mode of acquisition, the act whereby the transfer of property is effected.

Glossary

kinyan agav: the acquisition of moveables through the acquisition of real estate.

koves: laundryman, parallel to *katzar*.

malkut: the penalty of flogging.

mamzerut: bastardy.

metaltelin: moveable property.

metivta: college, school, parallel to *yeshivah*.

mezumanim: those invited to take part in a religious ceremony.

minḥah: the Afternoon Prayer.

miun: lit. 'refusal'; act whereby the marriage is dissolved of a wife who is a minor.

nahotey: lit. 'descenders'; Palestinian scholars who visit Babylon.

'orlah: lit. 'uncircumcised'; fruit of a tree in the first three years of its planting.

pitka: scrap of paper on which a legal ruling is recorded.

shamin: an assessment is made.

sheḥitah: the act of killing an animal for food.

Sheiyyah: a destructive demon.

Shekhinah: Divine Presence.

shema: 'hear' O Israel, the Jewish declaration of faith recited morning and evening daily.

shema 'ata: saying, ruling or discussion of the law.

shen: lit. 'tooth'; damage done by an animal while eating.

shilya: afterbirth.

shofar: ram's horn sounded on the New Year festival, Rosh ha-Shanah.

shomer ḥinam: gratuitous bailee.

shomer sakhar: hired bailee.

shufra: beauty.

simḥah: lit. 'joy'; sacrifices brought on festivals in addition to the *ḥagigah*.

sotah: a wife suspected of infidelity.

Stammaim: 'Anonymous Ones', the anonymous editors of the Talmud.

sugya: a complete unit of the Talmud.

talmid ḥakham: scholar, pl. *talmidey ḥakhamim*.

tefillah: the standard prayer recited thrice daily.

tefillin: phylacteries.

terefah: lit. 'torn'; a diseased animal, forbidden for food, or a human being whose condition is such that he cannot survive.

teyku: lit. 'let it stand'; the problem remains unsolved.

turgeman: interpreter.

tzarat ha-bat: rival (wife) of a man's widowed daughter.

Yerushalmi: lit. 'of Jerusalem': the Jerusalem or Palestinian Talmud.

yeshiva: college, school, parallel to *metivta*.

yetzer: 'inclination', lust.

Zohar: mystical commentary to the Pentateuch, end of thirteenth century.

zuz: coin corresponding to Roman *denarius*.

Notes

1 How much of the Babylonian Talmud is pseudepigraphic?

1 See J. Neusner's devastating but justifiable critique of earlier scholars in his *The Rabbinic Traditions about the Pharisees before 70* (Leiden, 1971), part 3, pp. 320–66.

2 *Cf.* the application of Neusner's methods to Amoraic material by his pupil David Goodblatt in his *Rabbinic Instruction in Sassanian Babylon* (Leiden, 1975), and in his article, 'The Beruriah traditions', *JJS*, 26, nos. 1–2 (Spring–Autumn, 1975), pp. 68–85. The form-critical methods of Neusner and Goodblatt are important, but neither has much to say on the pseudepigraphic nature of many Talmudic passages and on the contrived nature of a good deal of the Talmudic material.

3 This and the following instance have been noted, among others, by I. H. Taviob, 'Talmudah shel Bavel ve- Talmudah shel Eretz yisrael' in his *Collected Writings* (Berlin, 1923), pp. 73–88. For another interesting instance, see *Shabbat* 63b: 'When R. Dimi went up to Nehardea . . .'

4 Taviob in *ibid.* quotes this as an instance of the more dramatic and more fully developed literary style of the BT, as compared to the less complicated and less contrived nature of the JT.

5 See *Rashi.* The principle behind this ruling is that an ordinary partnership of this nature implies that both partners are employed as tenant-farmers by the owner and both are equally responsible for the work done in the field, as well as sharing the profits equally. Consequently, if, after the contract has been made, the Israelite agrees to work on his own on Sunday in return for the Gentile agreeing to work on the Sabbath, he is in fact asking the Gentile to work for him on the Sabbath and this is forbidden. If, on the other hand, the contract from the beginning stipulated that the Israelite would work on Sunday and the Gentile on Sabbath, each receiving the profits from the work they do, it is permitted, since then the Gentile is working on the Sabbath for himself, not for the Israelite. The final clause means that if no specific allocation of the days had been made, but after the work had been carried out the Israelite suggests that a calculation be made, i.e. the Gentile's profits are assessed against those of the Israelite, it is as if the Israelite is buying something of the Gentile's profits for working on the Sabbath which is, again, as if the Gentile works for the Israelite on the Sabbath.

6 The principle here is that, in the case of the Sabbath, it is forbidden since the Israelite may not himself work on the Sabbath, and hence may not benefit from the work done on his behalf by the Gentile. But in the case of *'orlah* there is no prohibition even for the Israelite himself to work on the *'orlah* trees, only to enjoy their fruit.

7 In a full discussion of the question whether there are fictitious *sugyot* in the BT, Abraham Weiss, *Le-Ḥeker ha-Talmud* (New York, 1954), ch. 2, pp. 181ff, refers to this passage in tractate *'Avodah Zarah*, as well as to the *sugya* in *Yevamot* 33b which the Tosafists understand to be fictitious, but Weiss denies that there are any *sugyot* 'made up' entirely out of the minds of the editors. For all that, Weiss is compelled to admit that, as the Talmud itself clearly states, the *discussion*, at least as given here and in *Yevamot*, is pure fiction. See my article, 'Are there fictitious *baraitot* in the Babylonian Talmud?', *HUCA*, 42 (1971), pp. 185–96, where I have argued that at least some of the anonymous *baraitot* quoted in the BT must have been invented for the purpose of elaborating on the Talmudic discussion. That this is so seems to me to be conclusive, even if one does not go so far as I. H. Weiss, *Dor Dor ve-Doreshav* (New York and Berlin, 1924), vol. II, pp. 242–4, who roundly declares that *all the baraitot* in the BT quoted in support of Amoraic statements *in the very same words as those used by the Amoraim* are fictitious or, if they are not, the Amoraim have plagiarised them. *Cf.* the *sugya* in *Shabbat* 76a where, at first, R. Johanan is reported to have 'said' something and later on in the *sugyot* it is suggested that he never said it.

8 This point is noted by J. Kaplan, *The Redaction of the Babylonian Talmud* (New York, 1933), ch. 13, pp. 148f. Kaplan rightly refers in this connection to the more than twenty instances (see *Berakhot* 9a and the parallels quoted in the marginal note to the Vilna, Romm edn) of, 'It was not stated explicitly but derived by inference', i.e. even where it is recorded as 'Rabbi A said, Rabbi B said' it does not mean that Rabbi A actually heard Rabbi B saying it, but he inferred it from an episode in which Rabbi B was involved so that Rabbi B *said* it by his conduct. *Cf. Shabbat* 5b where it is said that R. Johanan was only responsible for the basic law, but the actual formulation is that of later Amoraim.

9 Kaplan, in *ibid.* might have referred also to this passage, see *Rashi*, s.v. *gufa de-'uvda*, who uses the expression: 'It was not stated explicitly but derived by inference.'

10 This passage has been noted by, among others, Baruch Epstein, *Mekor Barukh* (Vilna, 1928), vol. I, p. 103. *Rashi* comments that the letter in the name of R. Johanan was quoted solely for the purpose of persuading the members of the household that it was forbidden.

11 This passage, too, is noted in *ibid.* The marginal note in the Vilna, Romm edn points to the curious fact that despite the claim in our passage that Rabbah only attributed the ruling to R. Jose, the *Tosefta 'Eruvin*, 4: 16, ed. M. J. Zuckermandel (Pasewalk, 1881), p. 143, does give the ruling in the name of R. Jose. It is possible that R. Jose's name was

added later to the Tosefta on the basis of the remark in our passage. In any event, it is stated explicitly here that Rabbah had no hesitation in attributing the ruling to R. Jose even though he never made it. Cf. *Rashi* s.v. *velo hi*, who understands the passage to mean not that Rabbah invented the whole ruling, but only that he invented the name of R. Jose and appended it to the ruling in the *baraita* because of R. Jose's reputation.

12 For a similar account regarding R. Hiyya, see *Gittin* 77a and the remarks of the Tosafists.

13 In this passage there is also an instance of, 'It was not stated explicitly but derived by inference'. It is said that there is no actual ruling by Rav but one can be inferred from Rav's conduct at his son's house. See *Ḥullin* 18b for the opposite idea that 'A did not say it' means that the rule does not follow his opinion, i.e. if he really did say it he did not 'say' it in the sense that it was not well spoken.

14 For a similar case where the names of the authorities were intentionally reversed, see *Kiddushin* 44b.

15 'Whoever repeats a matter in the name of the one who said it brings redemption into the world' (*Avot, Kinyan Torah* 6). Cf. *Yevamot* 97a: 'When a statement is made in the name of a departed scholar his lips move in the grave.'

16 See JT, *Berakhot* 2:1 (4b), on the need to state the name of the author of a ruling.

17 Cf. *Bava Metzia'* 109a, where R. Joseph quotes a ruling with such evidence of authenticity that three possible authors of it are mentioned and yet the Talmud concludes that there was never any such ruling, R. Joseph having invented it as a threat to his gardener with whom he had a dispute. See the remarks of the Tosafists. Many of the commentators to *Pesaḥim* 112a, 'If you want to hang yourself do it on a big tree', understand this to mean, 'If you want a ruling to be accepted by people, attribute it to a famous authority', i.e. even if he never said it. But, of course, the meaning of the saying is obscure, see the marginal note in the Vilna, Romm edn in the name of the *'Arukh*. In *Berakhot* 43b, R. Pappa gives a ruling in the name of Rava, but it is then suggested that Rava did not give any such ruling, R. Pappa having invented it in order to extricate himself from a difficult situation (but see the note of the *Baḥ* in the Vilna, Romm edn that evidently the *Rif* did not have this text). Cf. *Shabbat* 3a and the reference to Samuel's saying in *Shabbat* 107a. For a very illuminating example see *Shabbat* 68a where a statement is made by Munebaz. Munebaz here is not the name of a Tanna, but of the well-known king who was brought up among Gentiles (the subject of 'his' saying) i.e. the meaning is, 'Munebaz would say'. See A. Goldberg's review of A. Weiss in *Kiryat Sefer*, 31, no. 2 (March, 1956), p. 102. Cf. *Sifre, Shofetim* 168 on how wrong it is to change the names of teachers, attributing the saying of A to B and B to A. On the whole question, see the discussion in Israel Lipshütz's *Tiferet Yisrael* to the Mishnah (*Avot* 5:7, Vilna edn,

1913, p. 256, n. 49), and the lengthy erudite note by R. Margaliot in his Commentary, *Mekor Ḥesed*, to the *Sefer Ḥasidim* (Jerusalem, 1973), no. 577, n. 2, pp. 519–20.

18 Nahman Krochmal, 'Moreh Nevukhey ha-Zeman' in S. Rawidowicz (ed.), *Collected Writings*, 2nd edn (London and Waltham, Mass, 1961), ch. 14, pp. 243–4. Krochmal gives, among other illustrations, that of the Midrash (*Yalkut, Koraḥ*) where words are put anachronistically into the mouth of Korah which the author of the Midrash could not possibly have imagined Korah to have said.

19 See M. Friedmann's Introduction, part 4, to his edn of *Tanna de-Vey Eliyahu* (Vienna, 1904), pp. 27–44.

20 *Shabbat* 30b. The other *motif* in the tales is that of encouraging prospective converts and treating them with patience: see the conclusion of the passage. There is no intention of attempting to convey information about the lives of Hillel and Shammai.

21 It is well known, for instance, that in both Talmud and Midrash the Biblical heroes quote Scripture, for example in the dialogue between Abraham and Satan, *Sanhedrin* 89b where both quote verses from the book of Job. See *Shabbat* 30a where God, in a dialogue with David, quotes from Psalms, but see *Rashi*.

22 See *Rashi* and Tosafists that this is so is obvious since the whole question around which the *sugya* revolves is whether the husband is believed to render his wife forbidden to him.

23 JT, *Ketubot* 1:1 (24d).

24 See for example, *Yevamot* 96b where exactly the same expression is used.

25 See *Berakhot* 50a that this tractate was held to be especially difficult in the period of the Babylonian Amoraim.

26 *Makkot* 20a.

27 There is no actual reference to this practice anywhere in the Talmud, but the term *pitka*, a scrap of paper, is used in connection with a summons to the court, *pitka de-hazmana*. It is worth noting that none of these typical 'Babylonian' features appears in the much shorter account of the controversy in the JT, *Bikkurim* 3:3 (65c).

28 It is not possible to pin down the passage to any particular date but it is obviously Amoraic and, since it seems to be based on the account in the JT, it is probably late Amoraic.

29 Both A. Büchler, 'The conspiracy of R. Nathan and R. Meir against the Patriarch Simeon ben Gamaliel' in his *Studies in Jewish History*, ed. I. Brodie and J. Rabbinowitz (Oxford, 1965), ch. 6, pp. 160–78, and G. Allon, *Toledot ha-Yehudim be-Eretz Yisrael bi-Tekufat ha-Mishnah ve-ha-Talmud*, (Tel-Aviv, 1955), vol. II, pp. 72–3, appear to accept our passage as conveying, in the main, accurate information regarding the 'controversy' between the Patriarch and R. Meir and R. Nathan.

30 This phenomenon has been noted and discussed by H. Chajes, 'Mevo ha-Talmud', now published in his *Collected Writings* (Jerusalem, 1958), vol. I, end of ch. 17, p. 318; J. Schachter's English translation of Chajes

with notes, *The Student's Guide through the Talmud* (London, 1952), pp. 145–6; J. D. Wynkoop, 'A peculiar kind of paranomosia in the Talmud and Midrash', *Jewish Quarterly Review*, NS (1911), pp. 1–23; Epstein, *Mekor Barukh*, vol. II, part 1, ch. 1, pp. 690–2; Reuben Margaliot, *Le-Ḥeker ha-Shemot ve-ha-Khinuyyim ba-Talmud* (Jerusalem, 1960), pp. 5–14.

31 *Bava Batra* 67b. Other examples of the phenomenon in the Talmud are: R. Isaac Migdalaah giving a ruling regarding coins arranged like a tower (*migdol*) in *Bava Metzia* 5a; R. Zohamai ruling on the priestly benediction by a man whose hands are soiled (*mezuhamim*) in *Berakhot* 53b; Ben Rehumi discussing the case of a Nazarite vow having to do with the son (*ben*) of a friend (*reḥumi*) in *Nazir* 13a; R. Simeon ben Avshalom commenting on Psalm 3:1, *A Psalm of David, when he fled from Absalom*, in *Berakhot* 7b; Ayo reporting a teaching regarding a Sage whose destination on the Sabbath is uncertain (*ayo*, 'where he is') in *'Eruvin* 36b; R. Hisda remarking on certain acts as being of special piety (*middat ḥasidut*) in *Shabbat* 120a; *Bava Metzia* ' 52b and *Ḥullin* 130b; r. Haga commenting on people whose days are all like festivals (*ḥagim* in *Shabbat* 151b; *But to Benjamin he gave* (Genesis 45:22), R. Benjamin b. Japhet said . . . in *Megillah* 16a–b, and further comments by this teacher on the story of Benjamin; 'R. Pappa said: "For example, Pappa bar Abba" in *Bava Kama* 10b. In *Berakhot* 39b, R. Nahman b. Isaac learns that the name of a *tanna*, who conveniently turns up with a *baraita* which affords a way out of a debate between two teachers, is Salmon and R. Nahman observes: 'Thy name is peace [from *shalom*] and thy teaching is perfect (*shalem*) for thou has made peace among the disciples.' In *Bava Kama* 89a and *Bava Batra* 13b, R. Salmon gives a ruling that brings about peace in cases involving a dispute and in *Menaḥot* 29a, R. Salmon harmonises two Scriptural verses. R. Eleazar [the Amora] says: 'It is the teaching of R. Eleazar [the Tanna]' in *Shabbat* 19b.

32 Chajes, 'Mevo ha-Talmud', and in his note to the Vilna, Romm edn of the Talmud to *Bava Metzia* ' 25a, where he commends his observation as novel and 'true'.

33 Margaliot, *Le-Ḥeker ha-Shemot*. Margaliot rightly points out that in some of the instances the teachers are known for other sayings of theirs and that, for instance, other teachers are called Magdalaah (probably meaning 'from Magdala').

34 In the case of Ben Rehumi and Ayo, for instance, it is clear as can be that the names have been invented by the editors.

35 *Cf. Sanhedrin* 98b on the names of the Messiah: 'The School of R. Shila said: His name is Shiloh . . . The School of R. Yannai said: His name is Yinnon . . . the School of R. Hanina said: His name is Haninah . . .' Obviously here Margaliot is correct that the members of each School punned on their own Master's name and yet, even here, it is possible that we do not have an actual 'tradition' that the various Schools said what they did. The whole passage may be the result of editorial

composition (in praise of loyalty to one's own teacher?), the various Schools and their teachers being used as the heroes of a fictitious homily.

36 For example, the famous ruling of Samuel — *dina de-malkhuta dina* — is quoted as if he said it in a number of instances, whereas he only said it, in fact, in one instance, the others being supplied from there. See *Bava Kama* 113b, where the term *gufa* is used, and *Gittin* 10b; *Nedarim* 28a; *Bava Kama* 113a; *Bava Batra* 54b and 55a.

37 *Bava Kama* 119b; *Menaḥot* 76a; *Niddah* 63a.

38 *Berakhot* 59a; 60b; 69b; *Ta 'anit* 7a; *Megillah* 21b.

39 Isaac Halevi, *Dorot ha-Rishonim* (Berlin and Vienna, 1922), part 2, pp. 510f, rightly concludes that R. Pappa only said it once and the editors supplied it wherever suitable, since in *Berakhot* 59a the formula quoted by R. Pappa is also quoted as if it were known by tradition without reference to R. Pappa.

40 *Cf.* R. Jeremiah's problems in *Bava Metzia* ' 25a and *Bava Batra* 103a–b where the context is different but the wording the same, and for R. Ashi in *Bava Batra* 83b and 104b where the same method of quoting is used.

41 H. Albeck, *Mevo ha-Talmud* (Tel-Aviv, 1969), pp. 305–6.

42 See S. W. Baron, *A Social and Religious History of the Jews* (New York, 1952), vol. II, p. 306 and p. 433, n. 18.

43 *EJ*, vol. XI, pp. 1240–2.

44 See the continuation of the passage on R. Nehorai.

45 The whole passage in *'Eruvin* 13b deals with skill in debate. Note, for example, the number '48' in the arguments presented by R. Meir's disciple, Symmachus, which accords with the number '24' (twice '24') in the debate between R. Johanan and Resh Lakish in *Bava Metzia'* 84a (possibly corresponding to the twenty-four books of the Bible, as in Midrash Exodus Rabbah 41:5, but in any event a purely formal and artificial number). The statement (*Gittin* 56a) that Nero became converted to Judaism and R. Meir descended from him is probably also connected with a pun on *ner* and *meir* and perhaps based, too, on the fact that R. Meir's father's name is never given. Generally it may be remarked that R. Meir is a somewhat shadowy figure, though it would certainly be hypercritical to deny that he ever really existed. *Cf.* Midrash Ecclesiastes Rabbah 9:8, 'R. Zivatai in the name of R. Meir' — Zivatai from *ziv*, 'radiance'.

46 *EJ*, vol. II pp. 488–92.

47 The whole passage is full of hyperbole on the baseness of the *'am ha-aretz*, for example, the statement, so embarrassing to the medieval Talmudists, that it is permitted to murder an *'am ha-aretz* even on the Day of Atonement which falls on a Sabbath.

2 The Babylonian Talmud: an academic work

1 See Maimonides' famous statement in the Introduction to *Yad ha-Ḥazakah* (Amsterdam, 1702 and various edns), and see *Mamrim* 2:1 and *Kesef Mishneh*, that since the Talmud has been accepted as the final authority by all Israel, it is wrong either to add to it or subtract from it. *Cf.* Ch. Tchernowitz, *Toledot ha-Posekim* (New York, 1946), pp. 18ff, who asserts that it was the Geonim who virtually re-created the Talmud by converting it from an academic work into a Code of Law. On this whole subject, see Boaz Cohen, *Kunteros ha-Teshuvot* (Budapest, 1930; photocopy Jerusalem, 1970), pp. 18–25; Malachi ha-Kohen, *Yad Malakhi* (Jerusalem, 1976): *Kelaley Sheney ha-Talmudim*, no. 2, p. 1770 (that the *Bavli* is generally more authoritative than the *Yerushalmi*); H. H. Medini, *Sedey Ḥemed*, ed. A. I. Friedmann (New York, 1962), vol. IX, pp. 127–30; David Weiss Halivni, *Midrash, Mishnah and Gemara* (Boston, Mass., 1986), especially ch. 5, pp. 76–92.

2 For the use of the Aggadah for *halakhic* purposes, see the introductory chapter, 'Halakhah and Aggadah' in my book, *A Tree of Life* (Oxford, 1984) pp. 9–19, and for the use, in the Talmud, of *halakhic*-style argumentation even in the *aggadic* portions, see my article, 'The sugya on sufferings in *B. Berakhot* 5a, b' in J. J. Petuchowski and E. Fleischer (eds.), *Studies in Memory of Joseph Heinemann*, (Jerusalem, 1981), pp. 32–44.

3 On this, see my book, *The Talmudic Argument* (Cambridge, 1984), ch. 1, pp. 1–17.

4 On the redaction of the Mishnah, see Zecharias Frankel, *Darkhey ha-Mishnah*, ed. I. Nissenbaum (Tel-Aviv, n.d.); J. N. Epstein, *Mevuot le-Sifrut ha-Tannaim*, ed. E. Z. Melammed (Jerusalem, 1957), parts 1 and 2, pp. 9–494; H. Albeck, *Introduction to the Mishnah (Heb.)* (Jerusalem and Tel-Aviv, 1959); Weiss Halivni, *Midrash, Mishnah and Gemara*, ch. 3, pp. 38–65.

5 Of course the possibility cannot be ruled out that the *Mishnaic* material which purports to describe the procedures in Temple times really does go back to these times and is, therefore, practical; see Zevi Karl *Mishnayot Pesaḥim* (Lemberg, 1925), appendix 1, pp. 93–103, but apart from the fact that this material is small, when the Babylonian Amoraim discussed this material it had long been only of academic interest.

6 For example, *Shabbat* 1:1; 2:5; 6:1; 2, 3, 4; 7; 8; 9:5, 6, 7; 10; 11; 12; 13; 15.

7 See *Sanhedrin* 41a and 52b and Sidney B. Hoenig, *The Great Sanhedrin* (Philadelphia, Pa., 1953), excursus XXX, 'The abolition of capital punishment', pp. 211–13. *Cf.* the *mishnayot* in *Sanhedrin* on the stubborn and rebellious son and the 'devoted city', which, even if compiled at a time when capital punishment was carried out, can hardly have been anything but academic, *Sanhedrin* 71a and Mishnah *Makkot* 1:10.

8 Even the severely practical tractate *Niddah* contains material relevant only to Temple times, for example, 4:1; 5; 6:4; 11; 10:8.

9 Since most of the tithing laws applied only in the Land of Israel, see *Kiddushin* 1:9.

10 For example, *Yevamot* 2:6, 7; 3; 5:3, 4, 5, 6; 11:3, 4, 5, 6, 7; 14:4. *Cf.*
Kiddushin 3:9, 10, 11. *Cf.* the remarks of David Shputz, *Masekhet*
Yevamot Metzuyeret (New York, 1986), pp. 16–17, who quotes R. Shneor
Zalman of Liady, *Tanya* (New York, 1973), ch. 5, pp. 9–10, who gives
a mystical reason why the study of the Torah encompasses many problems of purely academic interest. Shputz continues: 'These holy words
of the *Tanya* are especially applicable to tractate *Yevamot*, in which the
Mishnah and the Gemara provide us with hundreds of illustrations on
the subject of levirate marriage and *halitzah* where it is also possible that
"this has never been and never will be", but, nevertheless, every law
in the Mishnah and the Gemara consists of the mind of the Torah and
the will of God.'
11 *Bikkurim* 1:5 and the whole of chapter 4 (which is not, however, part
of the Mishnah but derives from Tosefta *Bikkurim* 2:3); *Shabbat* 19:3;
Hagigah 1:1; *Nazir* 2:7; *Bekhorot* 6:12; *'Arakhin* 1:1; *Temurah* 2:3; 5:2;
Parah 5:4; 12:10; *Niddah* 3:5; *Zavim* 2:1; *Cf.* M. Guttmann, *Mafteah*
ha-Talmud (Breslau, 1924), vol. III, *s.v.* androginos, pp. 217–23. Even
if the *androginos* is not an entirely legendary figure, there cannot possibly
have been a sufficient number of these in existence to warrant consideration from the practical point of view.
12 *Nazir* 5:5; 6; 8:1.
13 *Makkot* 3:9.
14 *Sotah* 1–6.
15 *Gittin* 3:1; 9:5, 6.
16 *Bava Kama* 3:11; 4:1, 2.
17 *Sanhedrin* 51b and see the parallel passage in *Zevahim* 44b–45a. *Cf. Shab-*
bat 31a where the 'wisdom' and 'knowledge' of Isaiah 33:6 are applied
to the Orders of *Kodashim* and *Tohorot*, possibly meaning that, unlike
the other four Orders, these are largely for academic study, i.e. in order
to gain 'wisdom' and 'knowledge' alone.
18 M. Guttmann, 'Sheelot Akademiot ba-Talmud' in *Dvir*, vol. I (Berlin,
1923), pp. 38–87; vol. II (Berlin, 1924), pp. 101–64.
19 My study, *TEYKU The Unsolved Problem in the Babylonian Talmud*
(London and New York, 1981), examines in detail the more than 300
instances of this phenomenon, found only in the *Bavli*, never in the
Yerushalmi.
20 For examples of this kind of material see *Shabbat* 5b; *'Eruvin* 4b–5a;
25a; *Pesahim* 9b–10a; *Sukkah* 3b–4b; *Kiddushin* 6b–7a; *Bava Kama*
17b–18a; 26b–27a; *Sanhedrin* 79a; *Makkot* 7b.
21 *Kiddushin* 3b; 4b; 5a.
22 Of course the Torah was studied in Talmudic times for the purpose of
arriving at practical decisions. See, for example, *'Avodah Zarah* 19b,
on the disciple who has attained to *horaah* and one who has not reached this stage, and see all the Talmudic references to this or that being
the *halakhah*. But this is not really germane to our thesis which does
not consider mainly the aims and purposes of study in Talmudic times,

but the nature of the Babylonian Talmud as we now have it. The contention of this study is; (a) the Amoraim saw a major part of their activity in purely academic discussions, and (b) the editors of the *Bavli*, though interested naturally in practical law, had as their main purpose the production of a work of legal theory rather than a code of law.

23 Abraham Weiss has noted that the opening passage of practically every tractate is post-Talmudic, and this is supported by the similarity of language between them and the opening passages of *Kiddushin* and *Bava Metzia'* for the Saboraic origin of which there is a long-standing tradition, see Meyer S. Feldblum (ed.), 'Professor Abraham Weiss — his approach and Contribution to Talmudic scholarship' in the *Abraham Weiss Jubilee Volume* (New York, 1964), pp. 7–80 (English section), especially pp. 51–3.

24 Paradoxically, the *Rif*, whose aim it is to omit the purely academic discussions and give only the practical rules, is here obliged to consider at some length, by a casuistic process, what the actual law is as arising from the academic Talmudic discussion. *Cf.* JT, 1:1 (2a), beginning, where the practical question is raised, and see Rashi and Tosafists to *Berakhot* 2a here. A comparison generally of the *Rif* with the Talmud provides all the evidence required for our contention that the bulk of the Talmudic material is academic. The *Rif* extracts the practical material from the discussions, and when this is done it can be seen how small the practical material is compared with the theoretical discussions. There is, of course, no *Rif* at all to 'Zera'im (except *Berakhot*), *Kodashim* (except *Ḥullin*) and *Toharot*. On the idea that discussions about Torah are of great value even where there are no practical consequences, see *Ḥullin* 66b, *to make the Torah great and glorious* (Isaiah 42:21), and see Tosafists to *Bava Kama* 5b, s.v. *le-hilkhotehen*, and *Ritba* to *Yoma* 77b, ed. A. Lichtenstein (Jerusalem, 1976), p. 411.

25 The practical matter of the man who sleeps in a house without windows is artificial and has only been introduced in order to explain the *baraita*.

26 See my article 'The *sugya* on sufferings'.

27 See the *sugya* on intention with regard to the benedictions for wine and beer on 12a.

28 See the discussion of this *sugya* in my book *Studies in Talmudic Logic and Methodology* (London, 1961), pp. 65–7.

29 It is noteworthy that the *Rif* (p. 11b in the Vilna, Romm edn) simply records verbatim the initial law, omitting the whole discussion on it as irrelevant for practical purposes.

30 The *Rif* (13b–17b) does record, consequently, a good deal of this material.

31 The material in the *Rif* (42b–45a) is about a third of the Talmudic material in this chapter.

32 'Made to argue' because it is virtually certain that the explanation of R. Judah's distinction is editorial. It is in Aramaic whereas R. Judah's statement is in Hebrew.

33 There is some evidence that the rites of purification were continued long

after the destruction of the Temple, and that a quantity of the ashes of the red heifer were preserved for this purpose. Nevertheless, it is extremely unlikely that this is meant here.

34 It is generally accepted that the ending, 'The law is in accordance with Abbeye against Rava in the cases of *ya'al kegam'*, is a Saboraic addition and in no way demonstrates a practical interest on the part of the editors of the *sugya* itself.

35 *Cf. Kiddushin* 40b, 'They came to the conclusion that study is greater [than practice] since study leads to practice', i.e. and constitutes, therefore, *both* study and practice; see *Rashi* and *Ritba* to the passage, and S. J. Sevin, *Le-Or ha-Halakhah* (Jerusalem, 1957), pp. 204–12.

36 *Yoma* 26a; *Sotah* 7b; *Bava Kama* 92a (these last two are parallel passages, but the expression does not appear in the other parallel text, *Makkot* 11b); *Sanhedrin* 106b.

37 *Yoma* 26a (*Sotah* 7b and *Bava Kama* 92a are identical and only count as one).

38 *Sotah* 7b and *Bava Kama* 92a.

39 *Cf.* the tale in *Bava Metzia'* 86b, where a matter is debated between God and the Rabbis in Paradise. Rabbah, in the land of the living, is consulted and expires as he renders his decision. The problem discussed is academic not only because it takes place in Paradise, but would have been so even on earth since it concerns the question where there is doubt whether the white hair preceded the plague spot or *vice versa*.

40 JT, *Berakhot* 1:1 (1b).

41 The *Ketzot ha-Ḥoshen* (various edns) is an analytic work by Aryeh Laib Heller (d.1813), held by Talmudists of the old school to be a model of Talmudic dialectics.

42 Joseph Rozin, the Ragadshover Gaon (1903–8) was widely acknowledged as a Talmudic genius noted for his keen analysis of Talmudic concepts, as in his *Tzafenat Pan 'eaḥ* (Warsaw, 1958–36).

3 Rabbinic views on the order and authorship of the Biblical books

1 W. Robertson Smith, *The Old Testament in the Jewish Church* (Edinburgh, 1881), pp. 405–6.

2 S. R. Driver, *An Introduction to the Literature of the Old Testament*, 9th edn (Edinburgh, 1913), pp. i-ii, vi-x.

3 R. H. Pfeiffer, *Introduction to the Old Testament* (New York and London, 1941), pp. 41–2.

4 A. Bentzen, *Introduction to the Old Testament*, 2nd edn (Copenhagen, 1967), vol. I, pp. 24 and 32.

5 O. Eissfeldt, *The Old Testament An Introduction*, trans. Peter R. Ackroyd (Oxford, 1966), pp. 560–3.

6 M. Black and H. H. Rowley (eds), *Peake's Commentary to the Bible* (London, 1962), pp. 73–4. Among other modern works referring to the *baraita* and kindred topics are: C. D. and E. G. Briggs, *The Book of*

Psalms in the *International Critical Commentary* (Edinburgh, 1906), pp. xix-xx, liv; B. S. Childs, *Introduction to the Old Testament* (London, 1979), p. 51; Max L. Margolis, *The Hebrew Scriptures in the Making* (Philadelphia, Pa., 1922), pp. 20–4; L. Blau in *JE*, vol. III, pp. 143–4; M. Soloweitschik and M. Rubascheff, *Toledot Bikkoret ha-Mikra* (Berlin, 1925).

7 There has been considerable discussion on the dating and extent of the anonymous framework of the Babylonian Talmud, referred to throughout this book, see the literature cited in my book *The Talmudic Argument*, pp. 18–19, to which should be added: J. Ephrati, *Tekufat ha-Savoraim* (Petah-Tikva, 1973) and A. J. Avery-Peck (ed.), *New Perspectives on Ancient Judaism: The Literature of Early Rabbinic Judaism: Issues in Talmudic Redaction and Interpretation*, (Lanham, New York and London, 1989), and the bibliography cited there. For the 'two-source' theory of Talmudic redaction see Judith Hauptman, *Development of the Talmudic Sugya*, (Lanham, New York and London, 1988).

8 The Munich Codex (see R. Rabbinovicz, *Dikdukey Soferim*, New York, 1960) has, in fact, the introductory formula *teno rabbanan* also before the section on the order of the *Ketuvim*. It is not too clear whether the words *u-mi ketavan*, 'And who wrote them?', before the third section, belong to the *baraita* itself or are an editorial gloss.

9 Nahum M. Sarna, 'The order of the Books' in C. Berlin (ed.), *Studies in Jewish Bibliography in Honor of I. Edward Kiev* (New York, 1971), pp. 407–13, and see Sarna's article in *EJ*, vol. IV, pp. 827–33.

10 See *Bava Batra* 13b. Blau in *JE*, vol. III, pp. 143–4, takes it for granted that this is what the *baraita* means by 'order'. Cf. *Megillah* 14a, 'A Megillah written together with [the rest of] the *Ketuvim*', and see *Rashi*.

11 *Bava Kama* 102a; *'Avodah Zarah* 7a. For further examples of the use of *seder* in this sense, see *Shabbat* 89b; *Rosh ha-Shanah* 18b; *Megillah* 4b.

12 See, for example, the addition to tractate *'Uktzin*, and the 'happy ending' of *Berakhot*, *Yevamot*, *Nazir* and *Keritot*, and the reasons why *Shevu'ot* follows *Makkot*, *Nedarim* follows *Ketubot* and *Sotah* follows *Nazir* at the beginning of these tractates.

13 Krochmal, 'Moreh Nevukhey ha-Zeman', ch. 11, section 2, p. 114.

14 *Sanhedrin* 99a.

15 *Megillah* 31b, Cf. Tosafists who observe that the meaning is 'through the holy spirit', and see the note of Jacob Emden in the Vilna, Romm edn who remarks, 'The Shekhinah spoke out of his mouth', i.e. out of the mouth of Moses.

16 Here in *Bava Batra* and in the parallel pasage in *Menaḥot* 29b.

17 *Makkot* 11a.

18 *Tosefta Yadaim* 2:14, p. 683, and *Megillah* 7a.

19 See Driver, *Literature of the Old Testament*, pp. viii-ix:

> The entire passage is manifestly destitute of historical value. Not only is it late in date it is discredited by the character of its contents themselves. What are we to think of the statement regarding the authorship of the

Psalms? What opinion can we form of the judgement of men who argue that because a person (Melchizedek) happens to be mentioned in a particular poem, he is therefore in some way connected with its composition? Or of the reasoning by which Abraham is brought into relation with Ps. 89? . . . The fact of so much of the passage being thus unworthy of regard, discredits the whole. It is an indication that it is not the embodiment of any genuine or trustworthy tradition.

Driver is right that our *baraita* does not consist of any genuine tradition, but he is quite wrong in implying that it was *intended* as a genuine tradition. It *is* a wholly artificial construction but the artificiality is intentional and is on a par with general *midrashic* method, which, whatever else it is, was never intended as Biblical exegesis of any rigorous kind.

20 JT, *Sotah* 5:6 (20a). See M. Kasher, *Torah Shelemah* (Jerusalem, 1975), vol. XIX, pp. 363–6.
21 *Gittin* 60a.
22 See, for example, *Avot* 1:1, 'Moses received *Torah* from Sinai'.
23 See Tosafists to *Bava Batra* 15a s.v. *ve-'al yedey shlomo*, for a reading according to which Solomon was one of the 'elders' as in the superscription to Psalm 72.
24 *Midrash Tehillim*, ed. S. Buber, Vilna, 1891, p. 9, to Psalm 1:6.
25 See, for example, *ibid.* to Psalm 137 and the parallel in *Gittin* 57b: 'The Holy One, blessed be He, let David see the destruction of the First Temple and also of the Second Temple'.
26 Midrash Canticles Rabbah 4:4 and the parallel in Midrash Ecclesiastes Rabbah 1:17.
27 *Cf.* the commentaries in the Vilna, Romm, edn. of Midrash Canticles Rabbah by David Luria and Wolfe Einhorn (Vilna, 1878), neither of whom makes the suggestion that 'Ezra' here is the result of confusion between 'Ezra' and Ethan the *Ezra*hite. That *Ezra* is spelled with an *'ayin* and *Ezrahi* with an *alef* does not, of course, rule out the possibility that one was confused with the other.
28 See, for example, Midrash Ecclesiastes Rabbah 1:11 and Midrash Canticles Rabbah 1:10.
29 See *Megillah* 3a. *Cf.* Alexander Marx, 'Daniel's position in the Canon according to the Rabbis' in his *Studies in Jewish History and Booklore* (New York, 1944), pp. 1–2.
30 See Ibn Ezra's famous comment to Deuteronomy 1:2 and the 'hints' in his comment to Genesis 12:6; 22:4; Deuteronomy 3:11 and 31:9. According to Ibn Ezra, the whole of the final chapter of Deuteronomy, not only the last eight verses, were added by Joshua. *Cf.* the literature cited in my book, *Principles of the Jewish Faith* new edn (Northvale and London, 1988), pp. 232–57, and see Soloweitschik and Rubascheff, *Toledot Bikkoret ha-Mikra*, pp. 31–50.
31 See J. S. Lange (ed.), *Commentary to the Pentateuch by R. Judah the Saint* (Jerusalem, 1975). Later on this edition was withdrawn from cir-

culation and a bowdlerised version substituted with the 'critical' passages deleted. The references are in *ibid.*, pp. 64, 184–5 and 198.

32 Abarbanel, *Commentary to the Bible*, various edns, introduction to the Book of Joshua.

4 Literary analysis of the *sugya* in *Bava Kama* 11a–12b

1 Lit. 'Ulla said R. Eleazar said' i.e. Ulla heard it directly from R. Eleazar.

2 See *Rashi* and Tosafists for the meaning of *nitraf*.

3 The phenomenon is found throughout the Talmud. Taken at random, see for example, the lists of items in *Berakhot* 4b and 5a.

4 How much ink has been spilled, artificially to find a connection between the two sayings of R. Kahana or R. Nathan b. Minyomi in the name of R. Tanhum (*Shabbat* 21b–22a). And yet the sole connection is obviously because of this set of names.

5 Benjamin Kasowsky, *Otzar ha-Shemot le-Talmud Bavli*. (Jerusalem, 1976), s.v. 'Ulla amar R. Eleazar, vol. III, pp. 1144–5.

6 So, correctly, in the Munich Codex, current edns, 'R. Eliezer' obviously a copyist's error.

7 For Ulla and R. Judah see, for example, *Gittin* 19b; *Kiddushin* 38b, and the other sources quoted in Kasowsky, *Otzar*, p. 1146.

8 Hence, while in the *Bavli* the question is raised that R. Eleazar's saying is contradicted by the *mishnah*, in the *Yerushalmi* the question is, why state it since it is in the *mishnah*. In both the *Bavli* and the *Yerushalmi* the reply is that there are two Tannaitic versions.

9 The *Yerushalmi* uses the term *holekin* not *shamin* as in the *Bavli*. Perhaps the *Bavli* uses *shamin* because of the association with the other type of *shamin*.

10 See my essay, 'The numbered sequence as a literary device in the Babylonian Talmud' in Reuben Aharoni (ed.), *Robert Gordis Festschrift, Hebrew Annual Review*, vol. VII, (Ohio, 1983), pp. 137–49.

11 On contrivance in the structure of the *sugya* in the *Bavli*, see my book *Talmudic Logic and Methodology*, pp. 53ff.

12 Although this reasoning would not apply to the heirs, once the principle of mortgage has been established in relation to the purchaser, it operates in relation to the heirs as well, see Tosafists 11b s.v. *kigon*.

13 See *ibid.* end.

14 The original saying of Hezekiah is in *Kiddushin* 26a, to which this is a cross-reference.

15 It perhaps not without significance that sayings of Rava in particular are woven into the debate in our *sugya*, as are the two sayings of Samuel.

16 It is curious that in the parallels to this section in *Gittin* 21a; 78a; *Bava Metzia'* 9b, the same expression is used, *ve-hilketha*.

17 In *Kiddushin* 26a–27a the question is debated whether *tzibburin* is required and the conclusion (27a) is that it is not required. Consequently, this is a cross-reference to the passage in *Kiddushin*. Are we justified

in drawing the conclusion from this that *Bava Kama* was edited after *Kiddushin*?

18 It is surprising that there are three anonymous *baraitot* the different opinions of which fit so fortuitously into the pattern of the *sugya*. Weiss, *Dor Dor ve-Doreshav*, vol. II, pp. 242–4, has made the suggestion that all such anonymous *baraitot* are 'made up'. While this is far too sweeping, it is highly likely that the editors of the *Bavli* did, on occasion, create *baraitot* for the purpose of providing a dramatic framework to their material (see my article, 'Are there fictitious baraitot in the Babylonian Talmud?', pp. 185–96). This may be the case with regard to these three *baraitot*, especially to the less circumstantial and less detailed B and C.

5 Literary analysis of the *sugya* in *Bava Kama* 20a–21a

1 Lit. 'good things'. See *Rashi* for the two interpretations of *tehuma*, either as 'our vicinity' or as 'in our house of learning'. The expression is also found in *Bava Batra* 51a and *Zevahim* 2b. In the latter instance *Rashi* explains it to mean 'within the Sabbath boundary.'

2 The expression *zeh neheneh*, etc., is in Hebrew but the analysis and the rest of the framework is in Aramaic.

3 No mention is made of the fourth possible case, i.e. where B does suffer loss but where A does not benefit; see Tosafists 20a, s.v. *zeh*, and marginal note in the Vilna, Romm edn.

4 The idea seems to be that Rashi wished R. Hisda to look upon him as his teacher, at least for this purpose, and a disciple has to act as a valet to his master; see the remarks of Rabbenu Hananel in the Vilna, Romm edn., and of Chajes in the same edn. It is interesting to note that it emerges from *Berakhot* 44a that Rami was R. Hisda's son-in-law.

5 At this stage of the discussion the owner's loss is not taken into account, evidently because there is no payment for *shen* in the public domain. Thus the payment is not because the owner suffered loss, but because the owner of the animal has gained.

6 See Tosafists that the Talmud cannot mean that the owner has automatically and totally abandoned the food since, if that were the case, there should be no payment at all, the food no longer being his. Can the meaning be not that he has abandoned the food, but that the Torah has abandoned it in declaring that there is no *shen* in the public domain?

7 *Rashi* understands our passage to mean that the discussion is only on the case where B does not know that A resides in his premises and God always knows. But Tosafists cannot see why the case should be different where B knows of it.

8 Meiri to this passage, *Bet ha-Behirah*, ed. K. Schlesinger (Jerusalem, 1973), p. 65, follows his usual demythologising tendencies and understands *Sheiyyah* not as a demon, but simply as the ruinous state into which a neglected house falls.

9 Even though the orphans only suffered a small loss, in the whole *sugya* it is implied that even if B suffered the smallest loss A has to pay the rent, as in the case of the blackening of the walls. (Tosafists).

6 Literary analysis of the *sugya* on taking the blame on oneself

1 The reference is almost certainly to Rabban Gamaliel II since in the other account of Rabban Gamaliel and Samuel ha-Katan on the *birkat ha-minim* (*Berakhot* 28b–29a), Samuel ha-Katan is with Rabban Gamaliel at Yavneh. *Cf.* Frankel, *Darkhey ha-Mishnah*, p. 73, no. 1, and Mordechai Margalioth, *Entziklopedia le-Ḥakhmey ha-Talmud* (Tel-Aviv, n.d.) s.v. *Shemuel ha-Katan*, pp. 835–7, with the views of Aaron Hyman, *Toledot Tannaim ve-Amoraim* (Jerusalem, 1964), s.v. *Shemuel ha-Katan*, vol. III, pp. 1148–9, and Reuben Margaliot, *Margaliot ha-Yam* on *Sanhedrin* (Jerusalem, 1958), to our *sugya*, vol. I, n. 2, pp. 21b–22a, that the reference is to Rabban Gamaliel I, which involves the proposition that there was a Court at Yavneh in the days of Gamaliel I.

2 On the difficulty of Rabban Gamaliel being unaware of the interloper, since he himself had invited the seven, the Commentators give various solutions, for example, Rabban Gamaliel did not invite them personally but through a deputy (*Ran*) or Rabban Gamaliel said, 'The first seven of you to come up are the invited ones', and the question then was, who was the last man there (R. Hananel; Meir Abulafia, *Yad Ramah*, New York, 1971).

3 It is curious that in the passage which follows our *sugya*, with parallels in JT *Sotah* 9:13 (24b), and *Sotah* 9:15 (24c), it is similarly unknown whether the person to be identified is *Samuel ha-Katan*. Is he, in fact, a legendary person like Honi the Circle Drawer? If he is, it would account for the confusion as to his identity (see *ibid.*, that one reason he was called 'Samuel the Small' was because he was only slightly inferior to his namesake, Samuel the Prophet) and why there are no sayings attributed to him in the Tannaitic literature, except for *Avot* 4:19, which is only a quote from Proverbs 24:17 and has puzzled the commentators. (There is the suggestion that *Shemuel ha-Katan* in *Avot* is a mistaken decoding of the abbreviation for *she-harey ha-katuv*, 'for Scripture says', see J. Z. Lauterbach, following Bacher, 'Abbreviations and their solutions' in *Studies in Jewish Bibliography in Memory of Abraham Solomon Freidus* (New York, 1929), p. 145.

4 This expression is found also in *Ketulot* 103b in a different story about Rabbi Judah the Prince.

5 I.e. even though Shecaniah was not guilty of taking a foreign wife, he still said, 'We have broken faith'.

6 I.e. even though it was Achan who had sinned.

7 I.e. even though it is said in the previous verse (Exodus 16:27) that only 'some of the people' had sinned. Meiri (*Bet ha-Beḥirah* to *Sanhedrin*, ed. I. Ralbag, Jerusalem, 1974, p. 30) seems to have a different reading in

our *sugya*. Meiri's verse for Moses is: *Ye shall not do all we do here this day, every man whatsoever is right in his own eyes* (Deuteronomy 12:8), i.e. Moses included himself in 'that *we* do this day'. Incidentally, Meiri has a novel understanding of the taking-the-blame *motif*, seeing it as a form of indirect rebuke in order to avoid the offender the embarrassment that he would suffer from a direct, public rebuke.

8 *Rashi* to BT comments that Samuel ha-Katan said that he came there only to observe the procedures regarding the intercalation, but in the JT version he came simply to ask a question on a completely different matter. But see the suggestion of Abulafia *Yad Ramah* that, contrary to *Rashi*, the BT version may mean the same thing as the JT version.

9 See W. Bacher, *Aggadot ha-Tannaim*, Hebrew trans. A. Z. Rabbinovitz (Berlin, 1922), p. 63, n. 1, who identifies the culprit as R. Eliezer b. Hyrkanus, assuming that the editorial addition reflects actual conditions. J. Z. Lauterbach in *JE*, s.v. *Samuel ha-Katan*, vol. XI, p. 21, writes: 'Samuel was so humble that when during a controversy on the intercalation of a month to make a leap year, the Nasi asked an outsider to withdraw, Samuel, not wishing the intruder to feel humiliated, arose and said that he was the one who had come without invitation (*Sanhedrin* 11c).' The passage is 11a not 11c; there is no reference to a 'controversy'; and Lauterbach, too, takes the editorial material as factual. Margalioth, *Entziklopedia le Ḥakhmey ha-Talmud* is rather more circumspect, saying only that '*the Talmud adds* that it was not Samuel ha-Katan but someone else' (italics are mine). Eliezer Margaliot in *EJ*, s.v. *Samuel ha-Katan*, vol. XIV, pp. 815–16 is even more confusing: 'His modesty and greatness are best illustrated by the following incidents. When the patriarch Gamaliel II called a conference of seven scholars and eight appeared, he ordered the outsider to withdraw. Samuel, not wanting the intruder to be embarrassed, rose and said, "I am the one without invitation". Nevertheless, Gamaliel understood that it could not be him and ordered him to sit, praising him in very high terms (*Sanhedrin* 11a).' There is not a word in the passage about a 'conference', any more than there is about Lauterbach's 'controversy'. Even if the editorial material does reflect actual conditions (which, as we have shown, it does not), there is nothing in the episode to suggest that Rabban Gamaliel knew that it was not Samuel ha-Katan. On the contrary, the whole point of the story is that Samuel, for the best of reasons, tricked Rabban Gamaliel into imagining that he was guilty. All this is a good illustration of how a failure to distinguish between original material and editorial use of it in the Talmud can result in a distortion of the historical facts.

10 It is worthy of note that in all three stories the heroes 'stand up'.

11 *Cf.* the treatment of our *sugya* by Rabbi J. L. Bloch of Telz in his *Shi'urey Da'at* (New York, 1949), vol. I, pp. 152–7.

12 See *Rashi*.

7 Literary analysis of the *sugya* of 'half and half'

1 See *Shlomo Poliatchik, Ḥiddushey ha-'Illui mi-Meshet* ed. J. L. Goldberg (Jerusalem, 1974), pp. 8–9, for a different analysis of the arguments of Rav and Rav Kahana at this stage.

2 The Tosafists, *Ḥullin* 28b, s.v. *rav amar*, refers to *Ḥullin* 44b, where Rav examined a severed windpipe to see if the greater part had been severed, whereas here Rav holds that half is equivalent to the greater part. The Tosafists suggest that there the expression 'the greater part' may refer to half, or that the passage there follows the conclusion in our *sugya* that Rav agrees with Rav Kahana. It follows, in any event, that the formulation of Rav and Rav Kahana's statement is editorial and not original with them.

3 In JT, *'Eruvin* 1:1 (18b), Rav is quoted as holding that half and half is equivalent to the greater part, but there the formulation is simply: Rav said: 'If the act of *sheḥitah* was only on half [the organ] it is valid.' However, the JT continues, as in our *sugya*, that Rav agrees that it is invalid by Rabbinic law on the grounds of misleading appearances — *marit 'ayyin*.

4 See *Rashba* who remarks that Rav and Rav Kahana debate every case where there is a question of half and half and the greater part, and the expression regarding *sheḥitah* is only an illustration of the general principle. *Cf.* the note of *Ḥatam Sofer*.

5 The Tosafists *Ḥullin* 29a s.v. *de-kuley 'alma*, point to the very similar debate, *'Eruvin* 15b–16b, regarding an enclosure where the breach in the wall is exactly the same size as the built-up part. There, too, the analysis is in virtually the same words as here:' Did God say to Moses thus or thus?' And yet, as the Tosafists note, the contestants are not Rav and Rav Kahana, and the attempted proofs in each *sugya* are different one from the other. There is no reference there to half and half but to open and closed, suggesting that there the whole discussion is around the definition of an enclosure.

8 Rabbi Joshua b. Hananiah and the elders of the house of Athens

1 In Aramaic, *savey de-vey atuna*. From the reference to the young men seated higher than the old men, it is obvious that *sava* is used in the sense of 'sage', *cf. Kiddushin* 32b for this usage. The expression *de-vey*, denoting a house, has led some modern scholars to identify the place where the contest took place with the Athenium in Rome, but from the *midrashic* references to the intellectual superiority of the Jerusalemites to the Athenians (Midrash Lamentations Rabbah 1:2; 4; 5; 6; 7; 8; 9; 10; 11; 12; 13), it is clear that Athens is meant. The word *de-vey* is used because the Athenians have a special secret residence into which R. Joshua has to gain entrance.

2 See for example, R. Samuel Edels (*Ḥiddushey Maharsha*), the standard

commentator to the Talmudic Aggadah; the eighteenth-century Hasidic master, R. Levi Yitzhak of Berditchev, *Kedushat Levi* (Jerusalem, 1964), pp. 404–13; the nineteenth-century Rabbi of Slonim, R. Joshua Eisik Shapiro *'Atzat Yehoshua '* (Vilna, 1868) (photocopy, Jerusalem, 1969); and S. I. Hillman's Commentary to *Bekhorot* entitled *Or ha-Yashar* (London, 1921), pp. 12–13. R. Nahman of Bratzlav has a lengthy excursus on this *sugya* in his *Likkutey Moharan* (Bene Berak, 1972), n. 23, pp. 34b–45b.

3 See the article by Louis Ginzberg, 'Athenians in Talmud and Midrash', *JE*, vol. II, pp. 265–6, and the bibliography cited there and especially the translation and treatment by Bacher in his *Aggadot ha-Tannaim*, vol. I, pp. 122–6. Bacher rightly points out that the episode of the ship effectively rules out the supposed identification with the Athenium in Rome.

4 Genesis Rabbah 20:4, Theodor-Albeck, vol. I, p. 185.

5 Lamentations Rabbah 1:8 on sewing the millstone and Lamentations Rabbah 1:9 on the eggs and the cheeses (but here the Athenian produces the cheeses and the wise little boy the eggs). In both these it is a clever little Jewish boy who gets the better of the Athenium when the latter visits Jerusalem.

6 *Bistarkey*, rendered by M. Jastrow, *A Dictionary of the Targumim, the Talmud Babli and Yerushalmi and the Midrashic Literature* (New York, 1950), as 'cushions' and so by J. Levy *Wörterbuch über die Talmudim und Midrashim*, (Berlin, Vienna, 1924), but according to Levy the word is Persian. Rabbenu Gershom (followed by *Rashi*) renders it as 'thrones', which makes better sense. Perhaps the meaning is something like 'well-upholstered chairs'.

7 *Darbanai*, according to Jastrow, *Dictionary*, from the Greek, but Levy, *Wörterbuch*, refers to the Persian word *darban*, 'watcher' or 'doorkeeper'.

8 There is some confusion in the text here in any event, see note of S. Strashun (*Reshash*) in the Vilna, Romm edn.

9 In Aramaic *hakhimah de-yudai*. Cf. Midrash Lamentations Rabbah 1:19, where a little boy addresses R. Joshua ironically as *hakham shel yisrael*, in Hebrew.

10 Or perhaps the meaning is that the man was too good for the first woman of inferior family, see on marriage above one's station, *Kiddushin* 49a, 'I do not want a shoe too large for my foot'.

11 I follow here Bacher, *Aggadot ha-Tannaim*, but *Rashi* (followed by Soncino) understands it as referring to the lender not the borrower.

12 Lit. 'false things'.

13 Aramaic, *bey beliey*, 'place that swallows', see Soncino, p. 54, for various explanations, for example Scylla and Charybidis or a place in the sea that absorbs water or 'the well of Mirian'. The Soncino wrongly translates 'they', i.e. the Athenians, 'filled the jug with water' but this makes no sense. The text says that 'he', i.e. R. Joshua, 'filled the jug with water' in anticipation of the fate of the Athenians. Tosafists and *'Eyn Ya 'akov* have the reading here, 'In that place there are three images, one with

his hand on his head, the second with his hand on his heart, the third with his hand pointing backwards', possibly with echoes of the Colossus of Rhodes or the Pillars of Hercules.

14 For the possibility of certain interpolations into the Talmudic Aggadah, see Krochmal, *Moreh Nevukhey ha-Zeman*, ch. 14.

15 Bacher, *Aggadot ha-Tannaim*, points to the Persian words in the narrative, as above, and to the number sixty, the typical Babylonian unit of size, but it is in any event quite obvious that the passage is Babylonian.

16 Though it is possible that the divine name motif is introduced to demonstrate the superiority of the Jewish Sage who is not only a match for the Athenians at their own game, but has his own card up his sleeve so to speak.

17 *Bava Batra* 73a–74a. *Cf.* Marc Saperstein, *Decoding the Rabbis* (Cambridge, Mass., 1980), p. 232, n. 33, for a list of commentators to these stories. Saperstein rightly observes that from the various attitudes to these stories, it is possible to gauge the respective author's attitude towards the Talmudic Aggadah in general.

18 See ch. 1, above.

19 See my article, 'The numbered sequence as a literary device in the Babylonian Talmud', pp. 137–49.

20 See the remarks of Ginzberg, *Legends of the Jews*.

21 See Bacher, *Aggadot ha-Tannaim*, and Matthew 5:13. The sixty thrones in separate rooms seems to be an echo of the Septuagint legend and, as both Bacher and Ginzberg (*Legends of the Jews*), have noted, the unending pouring of the water seems to be an echo of the Danaides myth.

9 *Bavli* and *Yerushalmi* on Rabban Gamaliel and Rabbi Joshua

1 The military metaphor for learning is frequent in the Talmudic literature; see the examples quoted in my book *The Talmudic Argument*, pp. 8–9.

2 The 'interpreter', the more usual name for which is *amora* in the later, Amoraic period. Perhaps there are echoes here of the usage in the earlier Tannaitic period.

3 Reuben Margaliot, *Nitzutzey Or* (Jerusalem, 1965) p. 10, makes the very plausible suggestion that the references to 'in *Rosh ha-Shanah*' and 'in *Bekhorot*' are later, post-Talmudic references.

4 Parallel to *yeshiva* in Hebrew as in the JT version.

5 Probably a finely worked crystal glass, perhaps metaphorically to denote the vessel in which the wine of the Torah is imbibed.

6 *Mishnah Berakhot* 1:5.

7 *Contra* Soncino the meaning does appear to be tractate *'Edduyot*.

8 *Mishnah Yadayim* 4:4.

9 This is, of course, an editorial addition and is not found in the *Mishnah*.

10 The reference is to the special sprinkling water and ashes of the red heifer required for the purification of corpse contamination (Numbers 19). Rabban Gamaliel's position is authenticated.

11 The door of Rabban Gamaliel, as in the JT version, not, *contra* Soncino, to the door of R. Eleazar b. Azariah.

12 This, too, is obviously an editorial amplification, see the marginal note of *Masoret ha-Shas* in the Vilna, Romm edns, for parallels.

13 *Ḥagigah* 3a.

14 I.e. they made him head of the *yeshivah metivta*, but there is no reference in either version to R. Eleazar being appointed Nasi since he was not of the Princely House.

15 *Mishnah Zevaḥim* 1:3.

16 *Mishnah Ketubot* 4:6.

17 *Katzar*, corresponding to *koves* in BT. The incident of R. Zadok is in *Bekhorot* 36a. Here, too, Rabban Gamaliel waits until the shield-bearers enter the House of Study and here, too, R. Joshua says: 'If I were living and he dead.' It would seem that our *sugya* is an elaboration on the story (though not necessarily on the actual *sugya*) in *Bekhorot*.

10 *Bavli* and *Yerushalmi* on Rabbi Dosa and the Sages

1 The debate between the House of Hillel and the House of Shammai in this matter is recorded in the *Mishnah Yevamot* 1:4 to which our *sugya* is appended.

2 The translation of the JT version is mine, that of the BT is based on the Soncino though with a departure from it where necessary.

3 Lit. 'they surrounded him with *halakhot*', i.e. they cautiously led up to the subject.

4 *Teshuvot*, which seems to have this meaning here. The 300 arguments are mentioned in both versions. See *Rashbam* to *Pesaḥim* 119a, for the view that '300' in the Talmud in such contexts is an exaggeration. *Cf. Ḥullin* 96b.

5 *Medokha*, 'a mortar-shaped seat', Jastrow, *Dictionary*. *Cf. Tosefta Kelim, Bava Batra* 2:3, p. 592. The view of Maimonides that R. Dosa was a contemporary of Simeon the Just (introduction to his Commentary to the Mishnah and introduction to his *Mishneh Torah*) is evidently based on this passage, and the statement in the JT version that R. Eleazar b. Azariah resembled Ezra in appearance. But this would mean that R. Dosa lived for 400 years and, consequently, a number of scholars, even in the pre-modern period, took issue with Maimonides. See the Responsum of Sherira Gaon to this passage (B. M. Lewin, *Otzar ha-Geonim, Berakhot* (Haifa, 1928), p. 19) and Meiri to the passage that Dosa is not saying that he personally witnessed Haggai sitting on the mortar, but that he has the most reliable of traditions that this happened. *Cf. Kiddushin* 43a, where Shammai the Elder gives a ruling in the name of the Prophet Haggai. And see the standard encyclopaedias on Dosa.

6 Because the law of the Sabbatical Year does not apply to these lands, which are outside the Holy Land, for this purpose.

7 And there is no fear of the taint of bastardy (*mamzerut*). It is not clear

why Haggai should have testified to these three rulings particularly since they have no connection with one another.

8 I.e. you are not a scholar at all, although the reference would seem to be here and in R. Akiba's humble declaration to an inferior type of scholarship, a mere tyro in learning.

9 The reference is to the continuation of the verse, *Them that are weaned from the breast*, referring to R. Joshua's infancy.

10 A reference to R. Akiba the 'lion' of learning who was a poor man in his youth.

11 This is the correct translation (see Moshe Margolit, *Peney Moshe*), not 'his eyes are like those of Ezra' as some understand it.

12 There is no reference to Akiba's fame or to the golden couches in JT. In BT Jonathan seems to have his debate with R. Akiba alone, whereas in JT with all three Sages.

13 The Tosafists understand the three doors in the BT version as referring to the house of Dosa, in which case it is necessary to supply the information by implication that they met Jonathan, perhaps as they were leaving Dosa's house. In the JT version the three doors are in Jonathan's house. It is just possible that this is the meaning in the BT as well, though there is no explicit mention of them visiting Jonathan in his house.

14 But in the form 'she is permitted to marry a priest', i.e. she is like any other widow without the bond of levirate marriage which, when this is severed by *halitzah*, renders the sister-in-law forbidden to a priest.

15 At first in the course of the discussion and then, here, in the form *gufa*.

16 See Soncino for the suggestion of a rhyme in the BT version, *ah katan; bekhor satan; Yehonatan*, whereas the JT version simply has *bekhor satan*. See the continuation of the *sugya* in BT (*Yevamot* 16b) where a different exposition of the verse, 'I have been old', is given obviously because of the association with the story of R. Dosa. It is perhaps significant that the BT omits R. Tarfon because there are in the passage a number of 'threes': three Sages; 300 arguments; three doors; Haggai's three rulings; and, possibly, the three-fold rhyme of *ah katan; bekhor satan; Yehonatan*.

11 The Rabbi Banaah stories in *Bava Batra* 58a-b

1 On R. Banaah, see Louis Ginzberg in *JE*, vol. II, pp. 494–5, with a short bibliography; Hyman, *Toledot Tannaim ve-Amoraim*, vol. I, pp. 280–1; Margolioth: *Entziklopedia le-Hakhmey ha-Talmud*, pp. 178–9. Ginzberg renders the name as 'Banaah', but Margolioth reads it as 'Benaah' and, in brackets, as 'from Benaya'. The suggestion by Jacob Reischer ('*Iyyun Ya 'akov* in '*Eyn Ya 'akov* to the passage, edn. Vilna, 1890, 66b) that the Sage is so called because of his occupation as a grave marker (on the basis of Ezekiel 39:15, *u-vanah*) is ingenious but unlikely, since R. Banaah was a first generation Palestinian Amora and his occupation as a grave marker is only found in our, much later, passage. It is, however, just possible that

the name was given him by those who told the tale on the basis of the verse in Ezekiel. On the reliance on our passage for the view that the graves of the saints contaminate, see E. Languaer, 'Tumat Kohanim be-Kivrey Tziddikim' in *No'am*, 21 (Jerusalem, 1979), pp. 184–232.

2 See *Rashbam* on the basis of the comparison of Jacob with Adam.

3 *Cf.* Midrash Leviticus Rabbah 20:2, for the heels of Adam as brighter than the sun.

4 See marginal note that in some texts there is inserted here, 'The beauty of R. Kahana is a reflection of Rav; the beauty of Rav a reflection of R. Abahu', but Rav was earlier than R. Abahu which is why this is omitted from most texts.

5 *Amgushi*, a Zoroastrian Magus. The Soncino rendering of this word as 'magician' is misleading.

6 *Rashbam* understands it to mean that the *amgushi* used to dig up the graves in order to despoil them, but it is known that the Zoroastrians objected to burial in the ground as polluting the sacred element, see *Betzah* 6a and F. M. Müller (ed.), *Sacred Books of the East*, vol. VIII (Oxford, 1892), *Dinkard* 34:15, p. 106.

7 I.e. he wished people to think that he was only leaving a few barrels of various goods and hence he spoke in riddles, Meiri.

8 The meaning of the text is no doubt that the true son would have an inborn revulsion against desecrating his father's grave. On this kind of test in subsequent Jewish law, see I. Arieli, '*Eynayyim le-Mishpat* (Jerusalem, 1958), vol. III, *Bava Batra*, p. 175.

9 Soncino renders this as 'students', obviously understanding, incorrectly, the term *ḥaver* in its usual connotation of 'associate', which has no meaning here, where *ḥaver* simply means one of the company of thieves.

10 The word used here denotes an unearthly 'numinous' beauty, which makes sense of the comparison with the Shekhinah. *Cf.* the story of the *shufra* of R. Johanan in *Berakhot* 5b, where the reference is clearly to a 'numinous' beauty.

11 It is consequently precarious to conclude from all this that tractate '*Eruvin* was necessarily edited before *Bava Batra* and *Bava Batra* before *Bava Metzia*'.

12 See above, 76–9.

13 See, for example, Israel Katz, *Yalkut Pirushim* to *Bava Batra* (Tel-Aviv, 1968), pp. 571–3. The fierce debates in the Middle Ages between the Maimonists and the anti-Maimonists were, among other matters, about how strange *aggadot* such as this were to be understood. See Responsa *Rashba*, no. 418 (edn. Lvov, 1811), p. 65b; Abba Mari Astruc, *Minḥat Kenaot*, (ed. Mordecai Laib of Brody Pressburg, 1838), p. 69; Joseph Saracheck, *Faith and Reason* (New York, 1935).

14 See, for example, the lengthy passage at the beginning of chapter 3 in tractate *Berakhot*. *Maharsha* takes our passage literally and see *Ta'anit* 5b: 'Jacob our father did not die.'

12 The device of *addehakhi* 'just then'

1 Soncino translation, 'leave the school' is banal. *Geli* obviously means 'go in exile', see Abraham Schor, *Tzon Kodashim* in *Asifat Zekenim* (Jerusalem, 1972), *Menaḥot* p. 37b, for a far-fetched understanding, but this author, too, rightly understands *geli* as exile 'from ones home' not 'from the school'.

2 *Rashi.* See Tosafists, s.v. *o kum geli*, for the *midrash* that there are two-headed men living beneath the earth, and *Shittah Mekubetzet* on this. *Cf.* Ginzberg, *Legends of the Jews*, vol. IV, pp. 131–3, and the sources quoted in the notes, vol. VI, p. 286.

3 This follows Rabbenu Tam's understanding of the passage; see Tosafists, s.v. *shomea ' ani.*

4 This is the probable meaning of the statement that redemption is *per head.*

5 *Bava Kama* 11b.

6 *Berakhot* 48b; *Pesaḥim* 8b; *Rosh ha-Shanah* 24a; *Sotah* 4b; *Sanhedrin* 10b; *Ta 'anit* 25a.

7 *Kiddushin* 81a–b.

8 *Ḥullin* 6a, s.v. *ashkeḥey.*

9 See, for example, *Shabbat* 43a; 119a; *Kiddushin* 71a; *Sukkah* 52a; *Bava Metzia'* 110b; *Sanhedrin* 100a; *Menaḥot* 43a; *Ḥullin* 6a.

10 See *Berakhot* 18b; 51a; *Shabbat* 148a; *Betzah* 36b; *Ḥagigah* 5b; *Sotah* 49a; *Gittin* 7a; 11b; 16b; 31b; 45a; 56b; 62a; *Bava Kama* 112b; *Bava Metzia'* 22a; 59b; 86a; *Bava Batra* 16b; 22a; 149a; *Ḥullin* 105b; 110b; 111a; *Bekhorot* 27b; *Niddah* 26b.

11 This seems the probable meaning here.

12 For some reason *Baḥ* reads here *addehakhi ve-hakhi* which means 'during this time', but in view of the two *addehakhi*s in the same passage the correct reading here, too, would seem to be *addehakhi*.

13 Short for Abba Juden. Margaliot, *Nitzutzey Or*, p. 115, suggests that the name was abbreviated to Abdan ('destruction') because of the calamity which befell him.

14 They were minors, so that here there is another association with the original case of *ḥalitzah* by a minor.

15 For the conflict between the Nasi, Rabban Gamaliel, Rabbi's grandfather and the other Sages, see *Berakhot* 27b–28a, and above pp. 81–6. For the conflict between Rabban Simeon b. Gamaliel, Rabbi's father, and his contemporaries, see *Horayot* 13b. *Cf.* Allon, *Toledot ha-Yehudim be-Eretz Yisrael bi-Tekufat ha-Mishnah ve-ha-Talmud* vol. II, pp. 72–3.

Bibliography

Primary sources

Texts

Mishnah, ed. H. Albeck, Jerusalem and Tel-Aviv, 1957–9
Talmud Bavli, edn, Vilna, Romm, various printings
Talmud Yerushalmi, ed., Vilna, Romm, various printings; edn, Krotoschin, 1886
Tosefta, ed. M. S. Zuckermandel, Pasewalk, 1881
Sifra, ed. I. H. Weiss, Vienna, 1862
Sifre, ed. M. Friedmann, Vienna, 1864; ed. H. H. Horovitz and L. Finkelstein, Berlin, 1939; New York, 1969
Midrash Rabbah, Vilna, 1878
Midrash Genesis Rabbah, ed. T. Theodor and C. Albeck, Berlin, 1912
Avot de-Rabbi Natan, ed. S. Schechter, Vienna, 1887
Midrash Tehillim, ed. S. Buber, Vilna, 1891
Midrash Tanḥuma, ed. S. Buber, Vilna, 1913
Pesikta de-Rav Kahana, ed. S. Buber, Lyck, 1868
Yalkut Shim 'eoni, Warsaw, 1877
Tanna de-Vey Eliyahu, ed. M. Friedmann, Vienna, 1904
'Arukh, Nathan of Rome, Talmudic dictionary, various edns
The Mishnah, trans. H. Danby, Oxford, 1933
The Babylonian Talmud, translated into English under the editorship of I. Epstein, Soncino Press, London, 1948

Iggeret de-Rav Sherira Gaon, ed. B. M. Lewin, Haifa, 1921
Moses Maimonides, *Mishneh Torah* or *Yad ha-Ḥazakah*, Amsterdam, 1702 and various edns
    Commentary to the Mishnah in Vilna, Romm, edn of the Babylonian Talmud; ed. J. Kapah, Jerusalem, 1967
    Sefer ha-Mitzvot, Warsaw, 1883
    Moreh Nevukhim, Lemberg, 1886; *The Guide of the Perplexed*, ed. and trans. S. Pines, Chicago, 1963
Jacob ben Asher, *Turim*, Warsaw, 1886
Joseph Karo, *Shulḥan 'Arukh*, various edns

Bibliography

Encyclopaedias/dictionaries

Encyclopaedia Judaica, ed. Cecil Roth and Geoffrey Wigoder, Jerusalem, 1972

Entziklopedia Talmudit, ed. S. J. Sevin, Jerusalem 1947—

Jewish Encyclopaedia, ed. Isidore Singer, New York and London, 1925

Eliezer ben Yehudah, *Thesaurus: Complete Dictionary of Ancient and Modern Hebrew*, Jerusalem, 1959

Jastrow, M., *A Dictionary of the Targumim, the Talmud Babli and Yerushalmi and the Midrashic Literature*, New York, 1950

J. Levy, *Wörterbuch über die Talmudim und Midrashim*, Berlin and Vienna, 1924

Methodologies

Joshua ha-Levi of Tlemcen, *Halikhot 'Olam*, Warsaw, 1883

Malachi ha-Kohen, *Yad Malakhi*, Jerusalem, 1976

Mevo ha-Talmud, attributed to Samuel ha-Naggid, in Vilna, Romm, edn of the Talmud, after tractate *Berakhot*

Samson of Chinon, *Sefer Keritot*, ed. J. Z. Roth with commentary, New York, 1961; ed. S. D. B. Sofer with commentary, Jerusalem, 1965

Introductions

Albeck, H., *Mevo ha-Talmud* ('Introduction to the Talmud'), Tel-Aviv, 1969

Meilziner, M., *Introduction to the Talmud*, 4th edn with new bibliography by Alexander Guttmann, New York, 1968

Strack, H., *Introduction to the Talmud and Midrash*, Philadelphia, Pa., 1945

Variant readings

Rabbinovicz, R., *Dikdukey Soferim* (Latin title, *Variae Lectiones in Mishnam et in Talmud Babylonicum*), New York, 1960

Secondary sources

Abarbanel, *Commentary to the Bible*, various edns

Abulafia, Meir, *Yad Ramah*. New York, 1971

Aharoni, Reuben (ed.), *Robert Gordis Festschrift, Hebrew Annual Review*, vol. VII, Ohio, 1983

Allon, G., *Toledot ha-Yehudim be-Eretz Yisrael bi-Tekufat ha-Mishnah ve-ha-Talmud*, Tel-Aviv, 1955

Arieli, I., *'Eynayyim le-Mishpat*, Jerusalem, 1958

Ashkenazi, Bezalel, *Shitah Mekubbetzet*, Lemberg, 1837 and various edns

Astruc, Abba Mari, *Minhat Kenaot*, ed. Mordecai Laib of Brody, Pressburg, 1838

133

Bibliography

Avery-Peck, Alan J. (ed.), *New Perspectives on Ancient Judaisim: The Literature of Early Rabbinic Judaism: Issues in Talmudic Redaction and Interpretation*, Lanham, New York and London, 1980

Bacher, W., *Exigetische Terminologie der jüdischen Traditionsliteratur*; Hebrew trans. A. Z. Rabbinowitz, *'Erkhey Midrash*, Tel-Aviv, 1924
Aggada der Tannaiten; Hebrew trans. A. Z. Rabbinowitz: *Aggadot ha-Tannaim*, Berlin, 1922

Baron, S. W., *A Social and Religious History of the Jews*, New York, 1952, vol. II

Berlin, Charles (ed.), *Studies in Jewish Bibliography in Honor of J. Edward Kiev*, New York, 1971

Bentzen, A., *Introduction to the Old Testament*, 2nd edn, Copenhagen, 1967

Black, M. and Rowley, H. H. (eds.), *Peake's Commentary to the Bible*, London, 1962

Bloch, J. L., *Shi 'urey Da 'at*, New York, 1949

Briggs, C. D. and E. G., *The Book of Psalms* in the *International Critical Commentary*, Edinburgh, 1906

Büchler, A., *Studies in Jewish History*, ed. I. Brodie and J. Rabbinowitz, Oxford, 1956

Chajes, H., *Collected Writings* (Hebrew), Jerusalem, 1958.
Notes to the Talmud, in the Vilna, Romm edn

Childs, B. S., *Introduction to the Old Testament*, London, 1979

Cohen, Boaz, *Kunteros ha-Teshuvot*, Budapest, 1930; photocopy, Jerusalem, 1970

De Freiss, B., *Meḥkarim be-Sifrut ha-Talmud*, Jerusalem, 1968

Driver, S. R., *An Introduction to the Literature of the Old Testament*, Edinburgh, 1913

Edels, Samuel, *Ḥiddushey Maharsha*, in Vilna, Romm edns of the Talmud

Eger, Akiba, *Gilyon ha-Shas*; marginal notes in Vilna, Romm edns of the Talmud

Einhorn, Wolf, Commentary to Midrash Rabbah, Vilna, 1878

Eissfeldt, O., *The Old Testament: An Introduction*, trans. Peter Ackroyd, Oxford, 1966

Elijah Gaon of Vilna, *ha-Gra*; marginal notes in Vilna, Romm edns of the Talmud

Engel, J., *Gilyoney ha-Shas*, Jerusalem n.d.

Ephrati, J., *Tekufat ha-Savoraim*, Petach-Tikva, 1973

Epstein, Baruch, *Mekor Barukh*, Vilna, 1928

Epstein, J. N., *Mevuot le-Sifrut ha-Tannaim*, ed. E. Z. Melammed, Jerusalem, 1957
Mevuot le-Sifrut ha-Amoraim (Latin title: *Prolegomena Ad Litteras Amoraiticus*), ed. E. Z. Melammed, Jerusalem, 1972

Feldblum, Meyer S. (ed.) 'Professor Abraham Weiss — his approach and contribution to Talmudic scholarship' in the *Abraham Weiss Jubilee Volume*, New York, 1964

Bibliography

Frankel, Zechariah, *Darkey ha-Ishnah Rabbah be-Bavli*, ed. I. Nissenbaum, Tel-Aviv, n.d.

Friedmann, Shamma, *Perek ha-Ishnah Rabbah be-Bavli*, Jerusalem, 1978

Ginzberg, Louis, *Legends of the Jews*, Philadelphia, Pa., 1925

Goldberg, A., Review of A. Weiss in *Kiryat Sefer*, 31, no. 2, March, 1956, p. 102.

Goodblatt, David, *Rabbinic Instruction in Sassanian Babylon*, Leiden, 1975; 'The Beruriah traditions', *JJS*, 26, nos. 1–2, Spring–Autumn, 1975, pp. 68–85

Guttmann, M., *Mefteaḥ ha-Talmud*, Breslau, 1924
'Sheelot Akademiot ba-Talmud' in *Dvir*, vol. I, Berlin, 1923, pp. 38–87; Berlin, 1924, pp. 101–84

Habib, Jacob Ibn, *'Eyn Ya 'akov*, Vilna, 1913

Halevi, Isaac, *Dorot ha-Rishonim*, Berlin and Vienna, 1922

Hananel, Rabbenu, Glosses to the Talmud, printed in the margins of the Vilna, Romm edn

Ḥatam Sofer, novellae of R. Moses Sofer, Pietrikov, 1902

Hauptman, Judith, *Development of the Talmudic Sugya*, Lanham, New York and London, 1988

Heller, Aryeh Laib, *Ketzot ha-Ḥoshen*, various edns

Higger, M., *Otzar ha-Baraitot*, New York, 1948

Hillman, S. I., *Or ha-Yashar* to *Bekhorot*, London, 1921

Hoenig, Sidney B., *The Great Sanhedrin*, Philadelphia, Pa., 1953

Hyman, Aaron, *Toledot Tannaim ve-Amoraim*, Jerusalem, 1964

Ibn Ezra, Abraham, Commentary to the Bible, in various edns of the Hebrew text of the Bible

Jacobs, Louis, *Studies in Talmudic Logic and Methodology*, London, 1961
Principles of the Jewish Faith, London, 1964; new edn, Northvale and London, 1988
TEYKU: The Unsolved Problem in the Babylonian Talmud, London and New York, 1981
A Tree of Life. Oxford, 1984
The Talmudic Argument, Cambridge, 1984
'The *sugya* on sufferings in *B. Berakhot* 5a, b' in J. J. Petuchowski and E. Fleischer (eds.), *Studies in Memory of Joseph Heinemann*, Jerusalem, 1981
'The numbered sequence as a literary device in the Babylonian Talmud' in Reuben Aharoni (ed.), *Robert Gordis Festschrift, Hebrew Annual Review*; vol. VII, Ohio, 1983
'Are there fictitious *baraitot* in the Babylonian Talmud?', *HUCA*, 42 (1971), pp. 185–96
'How much of the Babylonian Talmud is pseudepigraphic?' *JJS*, 28, no. 1 (Spring, 1977), pp. 46–59

Kaplan, J., *The Redaction of the Babylonian Talmud*, New York, 1933

Karl, Zevi, *Mishnayot Pesaḥim*, Lemberg, 1925

Kasher, M., *Torah, Shelemah*, vol. XIX, Jerusalem, 1975

Kasowsky, Benjamin, *Otzar ha-Shemot le-Talmud Bavli*, Jerusalem, 1976

Bibliography

Katz, Israel, *Yalkut Pirushim* to *Bava Batra*, Tel-Aviv, 1968
Klein, H, *Collected Talmudic Scientific Writings of Hyman Klein*, introduction by A. Goldberg, Jerusalem. 1979
Krochmal, Nahman, 'Moreh Nevukhey ha-Zeman' in S. Rawidowicz (ed.), *Collected Writings* (Hebrew), 2nd edn, London and Waltham, Mass., 1961
Langauer, E., 'Tumat Kohanim be-Kivrey Tzaddikim' in *No'am*, 21 (Jerusalem, 1979), pp. 184–232
Lange, J. S. (ed.), *Commentary of R. Judah, the Saint* (Hebrew), Jerusalem, 1975
Lauterbach, J. Z., 'Abbreviations and their solutions' in *Studies in Jewish Bibliography in Memory of Abraham Solomon Freidus*, New York, 1929, pp. 142–9
Levi Yitzhak of Berditchev, *Kedushat Levi*, Jerusalem, 1964
Lewin, B. M. *Otzar ha-Geonim, Berakhot*, Haifa, 1928
'Rabbanan Savorai ve-Talmudan' in memorial volume for Rabbi A. I. Kook, *Azkarah*, Jerusalem, 1937, vol. IV, pp. 145–208
Lieberman, Saul, *Hellenism in Jewish Palestine*, New York, 1962
Greek in Jewish Palestine, New York, 1965
Lipshütz, Israel, *Tiferet Yisrael*, Vilna, 1913
Luria, David, Commentary to Midrash Rabbah, Vilna, 1878
Margaliot, Reuben, *Margaliot ha-Yam*, Jerusalem, 1958
Le-Heker ha-Shemot ve-ha-Khinuyyim ba-Talmud, Jerusalem, 1960
Nitzutzey Or, Jerusalem, 1965
(ed.), *Sefer Hasidim*, Jerusalem, 1973
Margalioth, Moredecai, *Entziklopedia le-Hakhmey ha-Talmud*, Tel-Aviv, n.d.
Margolis, Max L., *The Hebrew Scriptures in the Making*, Philadelphia, Pa., 1922
Margolit, Moshe, *Peney Moshe*, commentary to Jerusalem Talmud in Vilna, Romm edn of Talmud *Yerushalmi*
Marx, Alexander, *Studies in Jewish History and Booklore*, New York, 1944
Medini, H. H., *Sedey Hemed*, ed. A. I. Friedmann, New York, 1962
Meiri, Menahem, *Bet ha-Behirah* to *Bava Batra*, ed. B. J. Manot, Jerusalem, 1971
Bet ha-Behirah to *Bava Kama*, ed. K. Schlesinger, Jerusalem, 1973
Bet ha-Behirah to *Sanhedrin*, ed. I. Ralbag, Jerusalem, 1974
Müller, F. M., *Sacred Books of the East*, vol. VIII, Oxford, 1892
Nahman of Bratzlav, *Likkutey Moharan*, Bene Berak, 1972
Neusner, Jacob, *The Rabbinic Traditions About the Pharisees before 70*, Leiden, 1971
(ed.), *The Formation of the Babylonian Talmud: Studies in the Achievements of Late Nineteenth and Twentieth Century Historical Research*, Leiden, 1970
Petuchowski, J. J. and Fleischer, E. (ed.), *Studies in Memory of Joseph Heinemann*, Jerusalem, 1981

Bibliography

Pfeiffer, R. H., *Introduction to the Old Testament*, New York and London, 1941

Poliatchick, Shlomo, *Ḥiddushey ha-'Illui me-Meshet*, ed. J. L. Goldberg, Jerusalem, 1974

Raabad, Strictures by R. Abraham Ibn David of Posquirés to Maimonides' *Mishnah Torah* in various edns of latter

Ran, Commentary of R. Nissim Gerondi on tractate *Nedarim*, in Vilna, Romm edns of the Talmud

Rashba, Commentary of R. Solomon Ibn Adret on Talmudic tractates, Warsaw, 1883 and various edns
Responsa, no. 418, edn, Lvov, 1811

Rashbam, Commentary of R, Samuel b. Meir to tractate *Bava Batra* of the Talmud in Vilna, Romm edns

Rashi, Standard commentary to the Talmud by R. Solomon Yiṭẓhaki, printed at side of the text in practically all editions of the Talmud

Reischer, Jacob, *'Iyyun Ya'akov*, commentary to Jacob Ibn Habib's *'Eyn Ya 'akov*, Vilna, 1890

Rif, Code of R. Yitzhak Alfasi, appended to the Vilna, Romm edn. of the Talmud

Ritba, Novellae of R. Yom Tov Ishbili to tractate *Yoma*, ed. A. Lichtenstein, Jerusalem, 1976

Robertson Smith, W., *The Old Testament in the Jewish Church*, Edinburgh, 1881

Rozin, J., *Tzafenat Pen 'eaḥ*, Warsaw, 1903–8

Rubenstein, S. M., *Le-Ḥeker Siddur ha-Talmud*, Kovno, 1932

Saperstein, Marc, *Decoding the Rabbis*, Cambridge, Mass., 1980

Saracheck, Joseph, *Faith and Reason*, New York, 1935

Sarna, Nahum M., 'The order of the Books' in C. Berlin (ed.), *Studies in Jewish Bibliography in Honour of I. Edward Kiev*, New York, 1971

Schachter, J. *The Student's Guide through the Talmud*, London, 1952

Schor, Abraham, *Tzon Kodashim* in *Asifat Zekenim*, Jerusalem, 1972

Sevin, S. J., *Le-Or ha-Halakhah*, Jerusalem, 1957

Shneor Zalman of Liady, *Tanya*, New York, 1973

Shapira, Joshua Eisik, *'Atzat Yehoshua '* Vilna, 1868, photocopy, Jerusalem, 1969

Shputz, David, *Masekhet Yevamot Metzuyeret*, New York, 1986

Sirkes, Joel, *Bayit Ḥadash* in Vilna, Romm edn of Babylonian Talmud

Soloweitschik, M. and Rubascheff, M., *Toledot Bikkoret ha-Mikra*, Berlin, 1925

Strashun, S., Notes to the Talmud in the Vilna, Romm ed

Taviob I. H., 'Talmudha shel Bavel ve-Talmudah shel Eretz Yisrael' in his *Collected Writings* (Hebrew), Berlin, 1923, pp. 73–88

Tchernowitz, Ch., *Toledot ha-Posekim*, New York, 1946

Tenenblatt, M. A., *The Formation of the Babylonian Talmud* (Hebrew), Tel-Aviv, 1972

Bibliography

Tosafists, Standard glosses to the Talmud from the medieval French and German schools, printed together with text in most edns of the Talmud

Urbach, E. E., *Ḥazal*, Jerusalem, 1969

Weiss, Abraham, *Hitavut ha-Talmud Bishlemato* (English title: *The Babylonian Talmud as a Literary Unit*), New York, 1943

LeḤeker ha-Talmud, New York, 1954

Weiss Halivni, David, *Midrash, Mishnah and Gemara*, Cambridge, Mass., 1986

Weiss, I. H., *Dor Dor ve-Doreshav*, New York and Berlin, 1924

Wynkoop, J. D., 'A peculiar kind of paranomosia in the Talmud and Midrash', *Jewish Quarterly Review*, NS (1911), pp. 1–23

Zimra, David Ibn Abi, Responsa *Radbaz*, Lvov, 1811